Methodism

D1125211

LUTHER COLLEGE LIBRARY
University of Regina
Regina, Saskatchewan

RUPERT E. DAVIES

METHODISM

EPWORTH PRESS

To S.H.D. and J.M.C.

© Rupert E. Davies 1963, 1976

All rights reserved. No part of this publication may be reproduced, stored in a retrieval system, or transmitted, in any form or by any means, electronic, mechanical, photocopying, recording or otherwise, without the prior permission of the publisher, Epworth Press.

7162 0280 8

First published 1963
by Penguin Books
Revised edition published 1976
by Epworth Press
Room 195, 1 Central Buildings, Westminster,
London SW1H 9NR
Second impression 1982

Printed and bound in Great Britain at
The Camelot Press Ltd
Southampton

LUTHER COLLEGE LIBRARY
University of Regina

Contents

	Preface	10
1.	The Methodist Element in Church History	11
2.	The Eighteenth-century Setting	22
3.	John and Charles Wesley	38
4.	The Revival	56
5.	The Theology and the Hymns of the Revival	81
6.	Anglicans and Methodists	105
7.	Nineteenth-century Vicissitudes	113
8.	A World Church	135
9.	Modern Methodism	150
10.	The Prospects	184
	Bibliography	187
	Index	189

Preface

This book is written from the standpoint of British Methodism. It could have been written as well, or better, from the standpoint of American, or Australian, or many other kinds of Methodism. But since the standpoint is British, there are many omissions which non-British Methodists will deplore, but, I hope, excuse.

The last two chapters deal with many matters which are highly contemporary; I am myself personally involved in several of them. I have tried hard to be fair to opinions about them which I do not share, not least because many of those who hold them are my personal friends. Perhaps some of them will think that I have not succeeded.

I write as a convinced and lifelong Methodist who holds that Methodism has an important and permanent part to play in the universal Church of Jesus Christ. But Methodism did not flow in the blood of my forefathers in the way in which it did for many of my fellow-Methodists. I owe, therefore, for the writing of this book, much more than I can calculate to their influence upon me; and most of all to my wife, whose knowledge of the life of Methodism and conversations with me on the subject have affected me far more than she knows or would acknowledge.

Didsbury College, Bristol
June 1961

RUPERT E. DAVIES

For this edition I have re-written the last two chapters, to bring the narrative up to date, and revised the rest in the light of recent research. I am very grateful to those who have suggested various improvements since the first edition.

Nailsea
Bristol
June 1976

R.E.D.

CHAPTER ONE

The Methodist Element in Church History

It is quite wrong to think of Methodism as coming into existence in the time of the Wesleys. Methodism is, in fact, a recurrent form of Christianity, which is sometimes contained within the frontiers of the Church at large, and is sometimes driven, or drives itself, over those frontiers to find a territory of its own. Whenever it has gone into exile, both the Church from which it has been separated and the resultant 'Methodist' Church have been impoverished, and the breach has been difficult to heal. In the eighteenth century in England conditions within the Established Church were especially unfavourable for containing the Methodism of that age; and when the separation came it was soon evident that this Methodism had a vitality and range, a solidity and structure that its earlier manifestations had largely lacked. So this time the Methodist movement soon developed the qualities of a 'great Church', spread itself over the world, and took root wherever it spread. This expansion and permanence give the movement begun by the Wesleys the right to be called Methodism *par excellence*. The name originated with them, and that for which the name stands found its fullest and highest, but by no means its earliest, expression in their work.

If we take eighteenth-century Methodism as the norm, the dominant characteristics of this form of Christianity are at once clear, and can be simply set down. The first is a complete and whole-hearted acceptance of the cardinal doctrines of the Christian faith, as conveniently laid down in the historic creeds, combined with the conviction that doctrine which is not proved in devotion and life and does not issue in practical charity is valueless; in the last resort, 'experimental religion' (as John Wesley called it) is greatly preferable to doctrinal orthodoxy, if the choice has to be made between them. The second is insistence that the heart of Christianity lies in the personal commerce of a man with his Lord, who has saved him and won the forgiveness of his sins, and will live in him to transform his character. The third is stress on the doctrine of the Holy Spirit, the Person of the Trinity who is often neglected by institutional Christianity, yet without whom neither the fulfilment of the Lord's commandments nor the common life of the Christian community is more than a vague aspiration. The fourth is the earnest and patient attempt to embody the 'life in Christ', of which the New Testament speaks, in personal and social 'holiness', and the formation for this purpose of small groups of committed people who will encourage, correct, instruct, edify, and support each other. The fifth is the desire to make known the Gospel, and above everything else the love and pity of God for each individual sinner, on the widest possible scale and in the most persuasive possible terms. The sixth is a generous concern for the material as well as the spiritual welfare of the underprivileged. The seventh is the development of a Church Order in which the laity stands alongside the ministry, with different but equally essential functions, sharing with the ministry the tasks of preaching the Gospel, caring for the Christian flock, and administering the Church's affairs.

All through the history of the Christian Church there have been groups of people, large and small, who have exhibited all or most of these characteristics in such a way as to form a distinctive community within the larger community of the whole Church. These groups have not denied or decried the value of the liturgy or sacraments or ministry of the established or comprehensive Church in which they have arisen, any more than they have cast any doubt on its doctrines. Still less have they claimed to be the whole Church, or excluded other Christians from their fellowship. That is, they have not been 'sects', in the ordinary meaning of that word: they have not identified their own distinctive tenets with the 'full Gospel', or their own organization with the Body of Christ. Rather they have sought to be a Church within the Church—*ecclesiola in ecclesia*—with the function of stressing those elements of Christian faith and life which seem to them to have been neglected, and of taking Christianity as a whole with more seriousness, and therefore of incurring more personal cost, than the ordinary rank and file of Christians seem to do. This enterprise has usually involved strains and stresses, and often open conflict, with the hierarchy of the 'great Church', leading not infrequently to separation. After separation, men and women in these groups have been sorely tempted to regard the principles for the sincere application of which they have been cut off from their fellow-Christians as the be-all and end-all of Christianity, and sometimes they have succumbed; Methodism has sometimes become sectarian, and there are Methodists who are sectarian today. But on the whole the temptation has been successfully resisted, notably by the inheritors of eighteenth-century Methodism, who have never been properly described as Dissenters or Nonconformists, though they are happy to accept the title of a 'Free Church'. Only when the original vision has faded, temporarily or permanently, does Methodism sink to the condition of a sect. Otherwise it is for ever calling on the Church of which it is a part to be truly a Church; or, if the privilege of addressing that Church is withdrawn from it, it seeks to be truly a Church itself.

The earliest clear example of Methodism is the movement begun about A.D. 160 or 170 by a certain Montanus in Phrygia, one of the countries into which the territory of the modern Turkey was divided in ancient times. Phrygia was the traditional home of the orgiastic worship of Cybele, the 'Great Mother' goddess, who under various names attracted much of the religious devotion of the Middle East until the triumph of Christianity. Montanus is said to have been a converted priest of her cult, and therefore a eunuch. If so, he did not bring any of the ideas of his pagan past over into his Christianity, but he may have brought some of its fiery zeal, its proneness to ecstasy, and its tendency towards self-immolation. When he had become a Christian, he was strongly moved to counteract two perils which seemed to him to be threatening the very vitals of the Church. The first was Gnosticism, which offered to the spiritual and intellectual élite a special kind of *gnosis*, or knowledge, which made them familiar with the innermost secrets of the universe, and in particular assured them, in various ways, that the troublesome world of matter, including their bodies, was wholly divorced from the world of spirit. This meant a denial of the Incarnation of Jesus Christ, and was in fact a kind of elaborate spiritual snobbery which refused to ordinary people any access to the knowledge of God. The other peril was institutionalism, which, in the form of a tight organization presided over by bishops, was, in Montanus' opinion, throttling the work of the Holy Spirit.

Against these two evils Montanus came out with a new

'prophecy' upon his lips. 'The age of the Holy Spirit, promised by Jesus Christ, is here,' he announced, 'and I am His mouthpiece.' (He compared himself with a lyre which the Holy Spirit was playing.) Other prophets, mostly laymen, and including two eloquent women, Prisca and Maximilla, arose to confirm and amplify his message; and the community which was quickly created by their preaching sat down in the utmost simplicity of life and teaching to await the Second Coming of the Lord, which they expected rapidly to supervene on the new outpouring of the Spirit. The bishops of Phrygia and further afield took alarm, not at the content of their teaching—though Montanus certainly opened himself to misunderstanding by saying: 'I am come, neither as angel nor as ambassador but as God the Father'—but at the manner in which it was delivered, and at the danger represented by the new community to the settled and ordered life of the Church. Montanus and Prisca did not survive to bear the full brunt of the opposition, and Maximilla assumed the leadership. The bishops took united action against her and outlawed her followers from the Church.

Montanism in Asia Minor was broken up and gradually ceased, but its ideas and practices appeared in a more sober form a few years later in Rome. Here there was the usual opposition, but the decision of Pope Zephyrinus to excommunicate the Montanists seems to have been due as much to their hostility to a view of the Trinity which he favoured (though it was later declared heretical) as to any zeal for the truth or for proper Church Order. Once again driven out of communion with the Church at large, the Montanists continued in separate congregations. But in North Africa they could not be disposed of so easily. They produced several of the bravest martyrs who suffered in the dire persecution launched by the Emperor Septimius Severus in 203; there is no more moving story in the early history of the Church than that of the deaths of Perpetua, a young married woman of high birth, and her companions, many of whom were slaves.* These African Montanists had stayed within the Church and recalled its ministers to a higher notion of their vocation. They also brought the great Tertullian over to their way of thinking. His quarrel with the Church authorities became so outspoken that separation became inevit-

* It can be read in *Some Authentic Acts of the Early Martyrs*, translated by E. C. E. Owen (Oxford, 1927).

able, and the effect of his leadership among the Montanists was a greater and greater stress on austerity of life and on the control, not to say the elimination, of the passions. It is hard to say how long the Montanist communities survived in the various countries where they took root. Probably they were longest-lived in Africa, where there are traces of them in the time of St Augustine at the end of the fourth century.

Here we have most of the marks of Methodism: a religion which prefers personal converse with God to institutional forms and authority; a concern to bring the truth to simple people; a stress on holiness; a reaffirmation of the doctrine of the Holy Spirit; a semi-lay Church Order; and all of this combined with orthodoxy. It is true that attempts have been made to brand Montanism with heresy. But the charge is unconvincing, although one of the minor leaders, with a small group, was somewhat suspect on this score. (Has there ever been a Church of which this was not true?) Tertullian would never have joined a movement which had the slightest taint of erroneous doctrine; and he, Montanism's outstanding teacher, was not so much orthodox as one of the creators of orthodoxy.

But there were also grave defects: the claim to private revelations, difficult in any case to reconcile with a Biblical theology, led in the event to contempt of less self-confident Christians, and the passion for holiness became sour and moralistic, not least because of the attitude and teaching of Tertullian himself. In the end, Montanism leaves its mark on history as Methodism *manqué*.*

The Middle Ages provide at least two examples of Methodism, one of them wrapped in historical obscurity, the other widely known. All the information that we have about the Waldensians comes from hostile sources—as is indeed the case with the Montanists, but with consequences not quite so serious—and it is in any case scanty and confused. We may take it as fairly certain that Peter Waldo, their founder, was a rich man from Lyons, who insisted on knowing what the Bible said in his own language, and when he heard it, sold all his property and gave the proceeds to the poor. He then vowed to aim at the perfection of the apostolic life, and set out to preach his newly-found truth in the

* Montanism has usually had a 'bad press' in modern as well as ancient times. But there is a fair account of it in B. J. Kidd, *History of the Church to 461*, I, pp. 278–96.

countryside round about. Other laymen were moved to live and preach in the same way, and the itinerant preachers received the title of the Poor Men of Lyons. Waldo applied to the Lateran Council of 1179 for permission to preach, and was refused it; he preached nevertheless, and a Council of Verona, presided over by Pope Lucius III, excommunicated him and his followers. They therefore formed a separate organization, with a ministry of their own, but the ministers were authorized to celebrate the Sacrament of the Eucharist only once a year. A strict code of life was drawn up for those who wished to follow the Waldensian way. Bitter persecution followed, including a Crusade proclaimed against them, but it failed to suppress them; on the contrary it spread the movement over the mountains of Central Europe into Bohemia, Spain, Piedmont, and Lombardy. Their afflictions did not end with the Reformation, and they are best known to the English-speaking world by John Milton's sonnet which calls on the Lord to avenge His 'slaughter'd saints, whose bones Lie scattered on the Alpine mountains cold'.

So much is authentic history. But we cannot easily say what were their particular or peculiar tenets, nor even why they aroused such fierce hatred in the ecclesiastical authorities. They are freely called 'heretics', but their heresy seems to have consisted only in their disobedience to Papal authority, and there is no reason to doubt that they held the full faith of the Creeds. They approached the Bible, it would seem, in an over-literal way, and excluded penance, prayers to the saints, oath-taking, and killing (even in war), on the grounds that they were not approved in Scripture. Yet they surely exhibit many Methodist characteristics —the desire for apostolic holiness, lay preaching, concern for the poor and simple, personal religion, rating the call of the Holy Spirit above ecclesiastical rules, and at the same time acceptance of the faith of the Creeds. It is not without significance that at the present time the Waldensians of Italy work in close association with the Methodists of that country.

It is one of the puzzles of history that whereas the Poor Man of Lyons met nothing but obloquy and repression, the Poor Man of Assisi won his way with relative ease and speed to the approval of authority and the affectionate admiration of the contemporary Church (he was canonized two years after his death). One can perhaps conjecture that in the case of Francis the Roman Church was seeking to avoid the mistake made in the case of

Peter Waldo. The Waldensian Crusade began in 1209; it was in the same year or the following one that the Rule of Francis was officially approved by the Pope, Innocent III, who had ordered the Crusade. Certainly the life, the teaching, and the methods of Waldo and Francis were remarkably similar. Francis also was rich, Francis also sold his goods to feed the poor, Francis also gathered a group of followers and went from place to place to preach to simple people the love of God and the way of Jesus, Francis also understood and obeyed the Bible literally, and therefore renounced the use of force. Francis's movement, like Waldo's, was essentially a lay one, and, needless to say, Waldo and Francis would have agreed very well about the great issues of the faith and the character of the Christian life. There may have been profound differences also, but history does not record them. Waldo would willingly have served and died within the Church of his fathers; Francis was permitted to do so.

Francis did for his age what John Wesley did for his, and the resemblance between the work of the two men is all the more striking when the considerable difference between their personal characters and abilities is remembered. Wesley's preachers, laymen nearly every one of them, men of little education and no social standing, yet bringing out unsuspected gifts of eloquence and thought under the pressure of the Gospel, were not the first to tramp up and down the countryside to bring their message 'not to those who needed* them, but to those who needed them most'; the Brothers Minor, also many of them peasants, had done exactly the same thing five hundred years before, and at the same sacrifice of earthly comfort and repute. And when Wesley's preachers led the people to sing

> In the heavenly Lamb
> Thrice happy I am,
> And my heart it doth dance
> At the sound of His name,

they were expressing the same sheer joy in loving and serving their Lord as the 'Jongleurs de Dieu' who sang and prayed and preached and begged their way through the Tuscan hills. In essentials Francis and Wesley convinced their hearers of the same basic truths. Both of them knew and believed the theology in

* Wesley actually said 'wanted', but the word has changed its meaning, and 'needed' is what he meant.

which they were brought up (and Wesley at least treated theology with a high respect), and of course expressed it in the terms familiar to them; both of them had no compunction in indicating the pains of hell and the danger of falling into them. But the message that really went home from preacher to hearer when either of them was speaking was that God loved every man and Christ had died for every man.

Francis left home and possessions and prospects to find and follow the way of perfection, and attracted to himself those who were willing to attempt the same quest. Wesley's aim for himself and for his followers was similarly Christian Perfection. Francis saw, as Wesley later did, that holiness was most likely to be achieved, or rather given, through the life of fellowship, and both his preachers and the members of his Third Order were resolved to 'build each other up'. Nor did the preaching of the Gospel or meditation on the love of God ever monopolize the life of either Wesley or Francis, though each of them gave his unremitting care to both; what each of them did for the sick, the poor, the prisoners, and the oppressed would have filled the whole life of a normal Christian. Even their organizations were not dissimilar: much of Francis's *Rule* was repeated, *mutatis mutandis*, in Wesley's *Twelve Rules of a Helper*; when Francis divided Italy into 'provinces', each under a 'minister', he was anticipating the 'circuits' and 'superintendents' of eighteenth-century Methodism; and when Francis held a general chapter of his friars—of which Cardinal Hugolini said: 'Truly this is the field of God: this is the army, and these are the knights of the Lord'—and we are told that 'no vain or useless word was to be heard in all that multitude; each group of friars was engaged either in prayer, or saying their office, in weeping over their sins and those of their benefactors, or in reasoning on the salvation of souls'—the atmosphere was not very different from that of Wesley's Conferences. Yet Francis certainly exercised no direct influence on Wesley, who (in the ignorance of medieval piety universal in his time) said that Francis was 'a well-meaning man, though manifestly weak in his intellect'.)*

The Waldensians and the Franciscans are two recognizable examples of medieval Methodism, and there may, of course, be

* The resemblances between Francis and Wesley are drawn out in detail by H. B. Workman in his Introduction to *A New History of Methodism*, edited by Townsend, Workman, and Eayrs (1909).

others of which no adequate record has been preserved. It has been suggested that the Church of the Brethren (*Unitas Fratrum*), later known as the Moravians, was a movement of this type. The *Unitas* owed its foundation to Peter of Chelcic in Bohemia; he was so disgusted by the excesses of both sides in the bitter wars that followed the execution of John Hus in 1415, that he called on the more spiritual of Hus's followers to retire from political and national life and live in apostolic simplicity. One of his successors, Gregory, formed a community for the Brethren to live together in a place remote from the busy world and practise the Christian virtues in seclusion. To this end they broke away from the Papacy, and persuaded a Bishop of the Waldensians to consecrate a Bishop for them in 1467. Their seclusion did not protect them from savage persecution, either before or after the Reformation, except for a brief period in the seventeenth century, and after the Thirty Years' War they virtually ceased to exist as an organized body. The 'hidden seed' (as they called it) of their Church was, however, preserved by courageous individuals and groups, until in the early eighteenth century new life sprang up under the influence of Count Zinzendorf, and the whole Church of the Brethren entered on a new phase of existence.

There is nothing specifically Methodist, however, in the early history of the Brethren, nor in the Declaration drawn up in 1464 and accepted by the Church's first Synod in 1467. The whole emphasis of this document is on the quiet practice of Christian love among themselves, according to the teaching of the Gospels; no special value is set on doctrine, or sacraments, or ministry, or evangelism, or organization. The chief aim is to recover the practice and spirit of the Apostolic Church. Methodists of every age would, of course, agree with this aim, but would wish to go much further in several directions. Yet we know that John Wesley learned much from the Moravians and felt them, at least for a time, to be kindred spirits to his own. The truth seems to be that the impact of Zinzendorf was sufficient to change the character of the Church and make it Methodist, or at any rate to build a Methodist structure of faith and life on the foundations already provided. To the Moravians, in their Methodist phase, we shall have to return when we deal with Wesley's century.

The Lutheran Reformation provided a milieu in Germany and other countries where Methodism could arise and persist without being necessarily involved in conflict with authority. The form in which this took place in seventeenth-century Germany is called Pietism. The word nowadays implies among other things the requirement of withdrawal from the life of society as a whole, and a harsh judgement on secular values. But neither of these things belongs to the movement in its original nature. Philipp Jakob Spener, a Lutheran pastor until the end of his life, was primarily concerned to revitalize his own Church from within—to make it, as he thought, more truly Lutheran and Scriptural. He began religious societies, *Collegia Pietatis*, in his own house in Frankfurt, and brought many laymen into close cooperation with his endeavour to deepen and make more personal the religious life of his flock. Not everyone in high places in his Church applauded his aims, but he received much support from the Elector of Brandenburg, and lived to see the University of Halle founded as a centre for the propagation of his teaching. His chief theological supporter was August Hermann Francke, who, however, by his bluntness, brought other theologians into battle against him. In spite of controversy, pietistic views and practices spread far and wide in Germany, especially in the south-west, and in a diffused form exercised a profound influence on German theology right into the nineteenth century. Probably the greatest force in the extension of Pietism was wielded by the hymns of Paulus Gerhardt (1607–76), with their intense devotion to the Person of Jesus Christ and their serene confidence in the over-ruling love of God. Very familiar to English Christians is his 'O Haupt voll Blut und Wunden' (based on the medieval hymn ascribed to Bernard of Clairvaux 'Salve, caput cruentatum'):

> O sacred Head once wounded,
> With grief and pain weighed down,
> How scornfully surrounded
> With thorns, Thine only crown!

English congregations also sometimes sing his 'Befiehl du deine Wege', with its dauntless lines:

> Give to the winds thy fears;
> Hope, and be undismayed:
> God hears thy sighs, and counts thy tears,
> God shall lift up thy head.

Through waves, and clouds, and storms
He gently clears thy way:
Wait thou His time; so shall this night
Soon end in joyous day.

But probably only Methodists sing these stanzas from 'O Welt, sieh hier dein Leben':

My Saviour! how shall I proclaim,
How pay the mighty debt I owe?
Let all I have, and all I am,
Ceaseless to all Thy glory show.

Too much to Thee I cannot give;
Too much I cannot do for Thee:
Let all Thy love, and all Thy grief,
Graven on my heart for ever be.

It is not surprising that it was John Wesley in his missionary days in Georgia who translated the last two of these hymns, or that all these three hymns, and several others of Paulus Gerhardt, have been sung by English Methodists from the days of Wesley.

Here in German Pietism we have, unmistakably, the ingredients of Methodism—the distinctive type of Churchmanship which sets about reforming the inner life of the Church, the orthodoxy which is never questioned, but tends to remain in the background, the intensely personal devotion to God in Christ, the striving towards holy love, the groups which practise fellowship in the Spirit rather than in formal acts of worship, without neglecting the 'means of grace', the desire to make known the love of Christ to those who have passed it by, and, most plainly, the hymns. If it be thought that the Pietists did not always exhibit the same care for the bodies and minds of men as they did for their souls, we have to remember the University of Halle, and the poor-schools, orphanages, publishing-house, and dispensary founded by Francke. In fact, we are in an atmosphere here which is startlingly similar to that of the Methodism with which this book is chiefly concerned.

Yet Anglo-Saxon Methodism was not simply the recurrence of a religious phenomenon of deep and lasting importance which had appeared from time to time in the history of the Church. It was that, certainly, but it had complex causes and sprang from complex origins; and the setting in which it arose placed on it a stamp which makes it different from anything which has happened before or since.

CHAPTER TWO

The Eighteenth-century setting

The life of eighteenth-century England presents a series of startling contrasts—startling, that is, to us, but not, apparently, to those who actually experienced them. In the countryside, successful and progressive agriculture enabled the nobility and the gentry to build large and gracious houses, and to stock their tables, and often even their libraries, with all manner of good things. But the roads were shocking or virtually non-existent (Queen Anne once found it quite impossible to travel from Bristol to Bath), and the rural labourers lived in extreme squalor on bread, cheese, beer, and home-grown potatoes. In such towns as there were—and, outside London, only Bristol, Norwich, and in its own particular way, Bath, came anywhere near the modern conception of a town in the first half of the century—the merchants and the wealthier shopkeepers lived comfortably, not to say opulently. It is no one's business how their servants and other inferiors lived. And the streets which served all classes of the community were rarely more than twenty feet wide, with a carriage-way formed by rough blocks of stone and an open channel in the middle for garbage and slops. London, of course, exhibited these opposite features in the highest possible degree. Here was the centre of judicial and political administration, of commercial prosperity, of fashionable and refined living. A few yards away was the proliferating underworld of thieves, footpads, forgers, beggars, and harlots, sometimes as highly organized as the criminal area of Chicago at the most lurid point of its history.

Among the upper classes, culture based on a sound classical education was not only admired but practised on a large scale. Coffee house conversation, the drama, essay-writing, philosophy, and the less passionate forms of poetry flourished as strongly as they ever have in England. So far, it was an age of elegance, if not of creative achievement. But education, and therefore culture, was limited to one sex and a pitifully small proportion of the community. Even the members of that small proportion were not ashamed to dispose of their daughters by barter. The more civilized forms of sport (apart from bowls) had not been invented, and we must not criticize too harshly the addiction of high and low to cock-fighting and bull-baiting. But even the laxest moralist is disposed to comment on the immense sums of money won and lost at cards and dice, and on the widespread drunkenness of all classes of the community, with its attendant sexual promiscuity. London again set its own standards in gambling and inebriation, especially when the introduction of inferior gin changed the staple drink of the lower classes and made them drunk much more quickly and harmfully.

These contrasts became less sharp as the century advanced, because some of the slums gave place to more spacious residences and some of the prevalent vices were brought under control; and Methodism, as we shall see, had a far-reaching effect on the habits and morals of the populace. But much of this social progress was nullified by the growing effects of industrialization in the last third of the century. We are nowadays warned against speaking too specifically of an Industrial Revolution, but, Revolution or not, there is no serious doubt that the increasing demand for industrial labour herded masses of people into insanitary towns without reasonable accommodation, provision for health, leisure, or education, or any distinction between the working capacity of men, women, and little children.

It was the business of the Church of England to minister to the spiritual and moral needs—and, to a lesser extent, to the intellectual and social needs—of the people of England during this century, for this task had not yet been divided out among the various denominations, nor, of course, had the State come to carry through the works of charity which the Churches inaugurated. How effectively it performed its task will always be a matter of controversy. In one sense, it had all the facilities it needed. By the Clarendon Code of Charles II's reign, the Dissenters, finally defeated in the political field, had been degraded to the position of second-class citizens and no-class churchmen. The Toleration Act at the beginning of the reign of William and Mary had indeed restored to them the right to worship God in their own way, so long as their buildings were properly registered as Dissenting chapels and the doctrine of the Trinity was properly maintained inside them, and yearly Acts of

Indemnity protected them from punishment for breaches of the Test and Corporation Acts. But in private matters they were still subjected to vexatious persecution in respect of baptisms, marriages, and burials; when they appeared in public office it was very much on sufferance. (Sometimes, indeed, especially in the City of London, their fellow-citizens elected them to public office with the express purpose of prosecuting them afterwards for accepting it, or, alternatively, for refusing to exercise it.*) And no member of the public, even if he were himself a Dissenter, dreamed for a moment that the Dissenters had a 'mission to the nation'.

They did their best, of course, to maintain the life of their own congregations and to carve out a place for individuals and groups among them in the commercial and social life of the country. In both of these endeavours they gradually succeeded, but against stiff opposition. The excusable, but not very devout, practice of attending Holy Communion in the Parish Church just often enough to qualify for national or municipal office, was stopped by the Occasional Conformity Act of 1711. The Whigs, to their credit, resisted this measure, but the Tories forced it through. Deprived by their beliefs of a university education, the Dissenters set up academies to train young men for the ministry and the other professions. The Tories could not stomach this possible intrusion of Dissenting intelligence into Anglican preserves, and passed the Schism Act to dissolve every Dissenting place of learning. But at this point Queen Anne died, and the Act was never put into operation—so that the statement that 'Queen Anne is dead' still raises an echo in the minds of Free Churchmen who have any sense of history. Yet the academies continued thereafter under a threat, and though they often reached a standard of academic achievement much in advance of eighteenth-century Oxford and Cambridge, they did not encourage their alumni to attempt the conversion, or even the humanization, of England. The Dissenters gained the restricted ends of religious and commercial freedom for themselves by abstention from proselytization and by the quiet practice of their religion.

So the Church of England had the whole field at its disposal

* For instances of this see B. L. Manning, *The Protestant Dissenting Deputies*, pp. 119 ff.

—at least until the Methodists began to steal away parts of it. But it was in no state to take full advantage of its position. It was exhausted and impoverished (not financially) by the conflicts of the preceding century. Prolonged theological controversy, especially when it is confused with political issues and put to the arbitrament of the sword, leaves an inevitable aftermath in the desire to find a moderate and safe position which will command the assent (though not the zeal) of all right-minded men. More serious still was the loss of man-power, measured in terms of spiritual integrity and devotion and intellectual acumen. First of all the Puritans, perhaps something like half of the religiously alert members of the population (though not half of the population as a whole) had left, or been driven from, the ranks of the Established Church. Then the Non-Jurors, no less on grounds of high principle, and including in their small ranks several men who could have given great leadership to the Church as a whole, had gone. These were grave schisms within the one Church of Jesus Christ in this land. On the Church of England itself they had the effect of bloodlettings, and it is an indication of the spiritual poverty of that Church in the reign of Anne that an acrimonious bigot like Dr Sacheverell could be hailed as a champion of Christian truth.

It is not surprising that contrasts were to be found in the Church as extreme as those in society at large. Nor was there any machinery in existence at any time during the century for the exercise of a discipline which would have removed abuses on a wide scale, nor any force or personality to give unity of policy or thought to the Church as a whole. Rarely can a national Church have been so lacking in leadership and cohesion for so long a time. The chief cause of chaos was the failure of the Houses of Convocation to meet for any useful purpose until 1717, or to meet at all (except in 1741) after that. It is true that the Convocations had done nothing for many years—that is, since 1664, the last occasion on which the bishops and clergy met (to decide on the extent of their own taxation). But when they were revived in 1700 they had some chance of resolving the acute clerical dissensions of the time. The chance was lost in uninterrupted wrangling and recrimination between bishops and clergy. It might have been a disaster if they had continued to meet. It was certainly a disaster that they did not.

The result was that each bishop was left to do what was right in his own eyes in his own diocese. The bishops no doubt discussed their common problems over bottles of port in the House of Lords, but the result of their deliberations rarely reached the parishes. Since they had to spend two-thirds of the year in London for the execution of their political duties—owing their positions and hopes of higher preferment in most cases to the Whig politicians, they did not care to be absent from the House at voting time—and since their dioceses were mostly too large for proper visitations, even had modern transport been available, there is here no matter for astonishment. Confirmations, when they took place at all, were of vast numbers of people at once, and some bishops were so exhausted by the long ceremony that they resorted to the bestowal of a general blessing. Some bishops scarcely thought it worth while to visit their dioceses at all, though few, if any, were as remiss as George Hoadly, Bishop of Bangor for six years and of Hereford for two, and never seen in either place—but then, his writings show that he saw no real need for a visible Church, for orders, for sacraments, or for discipline.

The odd and pleasant thing is that there were many good bishops in spite of it all. Gilbert Burnet, whose origins were in the Church of Scotland, was Bishop of Salisbury from 1689 to 1715. His theology leaned to the side of broad rather than strict orthodoxy, but his administration and pastoral care of his diocese were above reproach. Joseph Butler was educated at the Dissenting Academy in Tewkesbury, but conformed in time to enter Oriel College, Oxford. He wrote the work for which he is most famous, The *Analogy of Religion*, while he was a parish priest in County Durham, and was translated in 1738 to the bishopric of Bristol, a post so poorly endowed that most of its holders regarded it purely as a stepping stone to a more lucrative appointment; Butler himself was compelled to eke out his income by holding the Deanery of St Paul's in plurality. He applied himself assiduously to the duties of his diocese; among other things he encouraged the 'Religious Societies' (though not, as we shall see, the Methodist sort) in Bristol itself, and obtained the passing of the Act necessary to establish a new parish in one of the mining areas of the city. He was offered the Archbishopric of Canterbury in 1747, according to reliable reports, and is said to have refused it on the ground that it was 'too late for him to try to support a falling church'. When he was promoted to

Durham for the last two years of his life, he left behind him in the Palace at Bristol a large number of new stone and marble chimney-pieces which he had installed during his residence there, and also 'a black marble altarpiece with a white marble cross thereon'—and thus aroused great suspicions of Popery among the sturdy Bristol Protestants of that era. Butler, with his strong desire for the orderly progress of the Church's life, worship, and thought, and his hatred of '*enthusiasm*',* which we shall have cause to notice later on, represented eighteenth-century Anglican episcopacy at the best it was able to reach.

Edmund Gibson, Bishop of Lincoln from 1716 to 1723 and of London from 1723 to 1748, would also have attracted attention even in a great age of the Church. Though he took more than the usual episcopal part in politics, and was the chief authority of the age on the constitution and laws of the Church of England, he yet had time to introduce considerable reforms in both his dioceses, to attend to his pastoral duties and to promote the welfare of the settlers on the American plantations (which were still in the diocese of London). He was even tolerant of the Methodists! And lest it be pointed out that these men, though honourable and conscientious, were scarcely heroes and martyrs of the faith, it is necessary to record also the career of Thomas Wilson, who was Bishop of Sodor and Man for no less than fifty-seven years, and hardly ever visited the mainland during the whole of that period. He refused better-endowed sees, even when he had been tardily released after wrongful imprisonment for suspending his archdeacon for heresy; and would not accept a single parish in plurality. He learned the Manx language, cared for his clergy, promoted church, school, and library building, and administered strict ecclesiastical discipline with complete impartiality.

So far as the parish clergy were concerned, we hear, of course, far more about the bad examples than about the good ones. No doubt there were many incumbents and curates who applied themselves diligently to the care of souls, and so attracted no attention to themselves and have obtained no place in literature. Perhaps it was clergy of this type who were willing to give Wesley and Whitefield a fair hearing when they visited their parishes. But even in the well-run parishes it was rare for the Sacrament of Holy Communion to be celebrated more than once a quarter

* i.e. fanaticism or religious hysteria.

(unless the parson was a Methodist), and there was often only one service on a Sunday. Since sermons were inordinately long for the most part, and not, if we may judge from contemporary pictures and descriptions, very carefully listened to, and in any case were sometimes repeated several times, it was perhaps not very serious that only one was preached on the normal Sunday.

When the clergyman was even moderately faithful he still could and did exercise a profound influence on all parts of the life of his parishioners. But many were not even moderately faithful, partly, at least, because the material conditions with which they had to cope were almost intolerable. Life was comfortable for the holders of rich benefices, and there is no excuse for the practice by which they accumulated several of these and then underpaid a batch of starveling uneducated curates to do their work for them in all their livings except one—and sometimes in that one also—while they were occupied in hunting, shooting, fishing, and drinking with the local gentry. But curiously enough, there were too many clergy, of all sorts and kinds, to fill the places available, and as a result beggars could not be choosers of the parishes where they would best serve God and the people, or, failing that, receive even a moderate stipend. Yet when the new towns began to appear in the last part of the century in the Midlands and the North, it was apparently impossible to provide clerical ministrations for their inhabitants, who grew up unchurched in their thousands. Of course, it is true that an Act of Parliament was required in every case before a new parish could be formed, and this involved a very cumbrous procedure, but a certain amount of leadership and initiative, at almost any level of the Church's life, could have modified some of the disastrous effects of this situation.

One more pair of contrasts falls to be noticed, this time in the intellectual and spiritual atmosphere. It was the great achievement of the so-called Cambridge Platonists, notably Benjamin Whichcote (1609–83), Ralph Cudworth (1617–88), John Smith (1618–52), and Henry More (1614–87), to take the heat out of theological controversy. Abandoning the relentless Calvinism of the Puritans, they stood for reasonable religion—for 'reason is the candle of the Lord'—and urged that the highest form of Christianity consisted in a mystical approach to God which in its later stages transcended reason and led the soul up to the knowledge of the Idea of the Good (which they were willing, in effect, to identify with the God and Father of our Lord Jesus Christ). In the last resort they were not intellectualistic, nor did they cast doubts on orthodox Christian belief; their purpose was to persuade the cultured world that Christianity was not really a battle of extremist dogmatisms, but a matter of insight and wisdom and love. But it was their insistence on the power of reason that most influenced their pupils, the Latitudinarians, who became almost the dominant school in Anglican theology for the first third of the eighteenth century. Men such as John Tillotson (1630–94) and Thomas Tenison (1636–1715)—they both became Archbishops of Canterbury—held that reason by itself could provide all that was needed in the way of divine truth, though its findings were confirmed by Scripture. This meant, in practice, a smaller and smaller emphasis on the distinctive Biblical doctrines, and a greater and greater emphasis on 'the truths of natural religion', and on the ethics which spring from obedience to conscience.

Thus the way was laid open, even in the highest circles of the Church of England, for the view that where revelation conflicted with reason, revelation must give way. Those who held this view have come to be called Deists, but many Latitudinarians did not believe very differently. John Locke (1632–1704) claimed to be a perfectly sound Christian, and was widely accepted, even hailed, as such. He professed to find in the Bible a simple natural religion on which all men of sense could easily agree. Miracles and particular doctrines could be left to the fanatics. John Toland's *Christianity not Mysterious* (1696) inaugurated the cult of Deism. He was careful not to repudiate any Christian doctrine that could give a good account of itself at the bar of reason; but the later Deists were not so tender, and the 'rational' doctrine of creation appears in Matthew Tindal's *Christianity as old as Creation* as the notion that God once created the universe and then left it to fend for itself.

These attacks on orthodox Christianity were not left unanswered. George Berkeley, later to become Bishop of Cloyne, having published between 1709 and 1713 *An Essay towards a New Theory of Vision, The Principles of Human Knowledge*, and *Three Dialogues between Hylas and Philonous* (works which, taken together, have been variously described as the matrix of idealistic philosophy and the quintessence of empiricism), turned his attention to one of his principal concerns, natural theology.

The result appeared in 1732, under the title of *Alciphron, or the Minute Philosopher*, and is a general defence of the Christian orthodox position, with an *a posteriori* proof of the existence of God, a demonstration of the reasonableness of the Christian revelation and of the value of public and private worship, and a refutation of the view that men are naturally virtuous. The book had a great vogue on its first appearance, but rather quickly went into obscurity. Opinions differ very greatly as to its merits, and secular philosophers tend to disparage everything that Berkeley wrote after 1714. But it was certainly regarded in its time as a powerful defence of orthodoxy.

More famous is Butler's *Analogy of the Christian Religion* (1736), which freely admits that Christian truths are not demonstrable, but only probable, and asserts that 'probability is the guide of life'. 'Let us compare the known constitution and course of things with what is said to be the normal system of nature; the acknowledged dispensations of providence, or that government we find ourselves under, with what religion teaches us to believe and expect; and see whether they are not analogous and of a piece.' So Butler outlines his purpose in the Preface, and goes on to show that the course of nature in human life and elsewhere is closely analogous to what religion, both natural and revealed, has to say about the work of God and the destiny of man. From the closeness of the analogy he argues to the probability of the Christian revelation. The style, urbanity, and skilful argumentation of the book have assured it a permanent place in English religious literature, and there is good reason to think that it countered the advance of Deism in its own time.

William Law, the Non-Juror, also entered the lists against the Deists. In his *Case of Reason* (1732) he is not so concerned as Berkeley and Butler to show that reason supports the Christian religion. In fact, he has comparatively little use for reason as such, uninformed by the Christian revelation. He holds that God gives the knowledge of Himself directly, through the feelings and through mystical apprehension, so that reason is not really necessary for the purpose.

These are only three of the manifold theologians who took it upon themselves to refute the Deists and the Rationalists; but for the most part the reading of them is as arid an occupation as the reading of the Deistic works. Not all of them together succeeded in dispelling the cold mist of doubt that for more than half a century hung over the specifically Christian doctrines in the minds even of those who were pledged to preach them. Even Butler and Berkeley in their defence of orthodoxy granted to the 'men of reason' many of their premises. Only Law brought a little warmth into the atmosphere, and he stood outside the main line of Anglican thought. So the general run of preachers took the safest course, and contented themselves with instilling morality, on the principles of which all parties agreed, Christians and Rationalists alike. The theological climate was exceedingly bleak, and religiously there was almost a vacuum.

Yet here again there was a partial compensation, provided by the 'Religious Societies'. About the year 1676 a certain Dr Anthony Horneck gathered together a group of young men in London who wished to 'apply themselves to good discourse and to things wherein they might edify one another'. Other groups grew out of the original one, and two years later a member of one of the groups published *The Country Parson's Advice to his Parishioners*, a book later highly prized by the members of the Holy Club under John Wesley's leadership. We know* the rules that governed these early Societies as they were drawn up by Dr Horneck. 'All that enter the Society shall resolve upon a holy and serious life' is the first of all. Then it is laid down that only those confirmed by a bishop are eligible—no Dissenters allowed—and that a minister of the Church of England should in all cases be the appointed director. Several likely subjects were barred from discussion at the meetings of the Societies—controverted points of divinity, for instance, and the government of Church and State. In fact, the meetings were to be made up mostly of the reciting of liturgical prayers and the reading of books of 'practical divinity'. If time allowed, a psalm might be sung, and those who were so disposed might discourse with one another about their spiritual concerns; but it was expressly laid down that such discourse was not to be 'a standing exercise which any shall be obliged to attend unto'. Every member contributed sixpence a week if present, and threepence if absent; if he resigned, five shillings were due from him. The final Rule indicates the kind of conduct that was expected from members: 'To love one another. When reviled, not to revile again. To speak evil of no man. To wrong no man. To pray, if possible, seven times a

* From the life of Anthony Horneck in Hone's *Lives of Eminent Christians*, I, pp. 309, 310.

day. To keep close to the Church of England. To transact all things peaceably and gently. To be helpful to each other. To use themselves to holy thoughts in their coming in and going out. To examine themselves every night. To give everyone their due. To obey superiors, both spiritual and temporal.'

It is not easy to estimate the size and growth of these Societies, since the promoters of such movements tend to exaggerate their success, but Josiah Woodward's *Account of the Rise and Progress of the Religious Societies* (fourth edition, 1712) shows clearly that expansion and development went on into the eighteenth century. It also gives the Rules for Woodward's own Society in Poplar. These are basically the same as Horneck's; we are told, for instance, that the sole design of the Society is 'to promote real holiness of heart and life'; and there is the same close connection with the Church of England, and the same prohibition of discussion about controversial theology and the government of Church and State. But there are additional provisions: every member of the Society is 'to express due Christian charity, candour, and moderation towards all such Dissenters as are of good conversation'; and he is to abstain from 'lewd playhouses', and from 'all unnecessary resort to public houses and taverns', in view of 'the scandal of being concerned in those games which are used' in such places. As in the earlier Societies, money was collected from the members for the purposes of charity. The most significant differences are that in the absence of the director of the Society (always an ordained minister) a specially appointed 'steward', a layman, was to take charge of the meeting; and that the part played by conversation on spiritual matters, which was to take place half-way through the devotional exercises, was greatly enhanced.

Another kind of Society was probably an offshot from the Religious Societies, or at least resulted from the same spiritual impetus. In 1698 Dr Thomas Bray formed the Society for the Promotion of Christian Knowledge. Its aim was to provide schools in London where the catechism could be taught to children not normally within the reach of the Church; to print good books for the poor; and to promote religion in the American plantations by means, mostly, of suitable literature. Bray went to America to further the purposes of his Society, and on his return from Maryland decided that another Society, especially designed to assist the evangelization of countries other than England, was necessary. In 1701 the Society for the Propagation of the Gospel in Foreign Parts was incorporated by royal charter. Its emissaries were first of all to establish in the faith the English workers on the plantations and in the other areas of the colonial empire, and then to bend their attention to the conversion of the natives. It is easy enough to smile, or even to jeer, at the paternalism of the conception which lies behind both societies, but it is quite certain that unless people with a paternal desire to spread the blessings of the Gospel among the underprivileged had taken the matter in hand, no one would have done so at all.

Equally philanthropic in intention, but much less agreeable in method, was the Society for the Reformation of Manners, founded in 1692. The civil disturbances of the century, the swift changes of government, the reaction against the Puritan attempt to control the private lives of English people, and the unseemly example of the Court, had led to the open and widespread flouting of the laws against blasphemy, profanation of the Sabbath, and to breaches of public morality. Instead of pressing for changes in the laws which would have brought them into step with contemporary morality—which is the method widely recommended today in similar circumstances—the Society determined to have the law enforced. It therefore employed an army of informers to discover instances of lawbreaking—not, apparently, a very difficult assignment—and to bring the offenders before the courts. The prosecutions usually succeeded, but not with any substantial advantage to the cause of real morality. For all their snooping, these do-gooders undoubtedly had the welfare of the nation at heart; their defect was that they had not seen that enforced obedience to the law is not to be equated with Christian ethics.

* * *

Such was the Anglicanism, with its strength and weakness, in which John Wesley and the eighteenth-century Methodists were nurtured. Wesley never ceased to praise and admire the government, the institutions, the liturgy, and the doctrine of the Church of England as he knew it. Yet it is plain that we cannot ascribe the development of his spiritual genius and the formulation of his theology, still less his evangelical zeal, solely to the nurture and influence of his mother Church as it was in the eighteenth century. Of course, like devout Anglicans of all centuries, he went back to the springs of his Church's spiritual life, and we know that he learned much from Thomas à Kempis and from Jeremy Taylor's *Holy Living* and *Holy Dying*—two Anglican classics and one adopted Anglican classic. Much came to him from Martin Luther (with whom, however, he strongly disagreed on certain points) and from John Calvin (in spite of the rejection of his central tenet of predestination). Still more came from the voluminous writings of the Puritan divines who had sustained his forefathers on both his mother's and father's side, and who are well represented by such people as John Owen, Henry Scougal, and Richard and Joseph Alleine in the 'Christian Library' which he published. But there were also two strong eighteenth-century influences, playing upon him from outside the Church of England, without a full account of which any description of the background of Methodism would be seriously inadequate.

William Law (1686–1761) was qualified to occupy a very lofty position either in the ecclesiastical or in the academic world. He was ordained and became a Fellow of Emmanuel College, Cambridge, in 1711, but when Queen Anne died and George I acceded he found it impossible, on conscientious grounds, to swear the oath of allegiance to the new monarch, and lost his Fellowship. He spent part of the rest of his life as tutor to the father of Edward Gibbon the historian, but most of it in retirement, devoting himself to meditation, writing, and the organization of schools and almhouses. In his later years, under the influence of Jakob Böehme, he leaned heavily towards mysticism and grew further away from the Church of his birth; but in middle life he published two books which were profound in their effect on those Anglicans who were willing to take the ethical teaching of their Church with complete seriousness and follow it through to the end.

The first of the two was a *Treatise on Christian Perfection*, published in 1726. It is quite drastic in its demands for the renunciation by the Christian of 'all those Enjoyments and Indulgences, which may make us less able and less disposed to improve and cooperate with those Degrees of Divine Grace, that are communicated to us'. Such 'indulgences include the peaceful and pleasurable enjoyment of riches', which, says Law, is 'everywhere condemned by our Blessed Saviour'. The only purpose of riches is that we should use them to relieve the poor. Yet such

Moravians). Those who lived on the estate formed themselves—under the joint guidance of Zinzendorf and their Moravian pastors, together with the Pietist Johann Andreas Rothe, whom Zinzendorf appointed to be head pastor—into a closely-knit religious community. Zinzendorf gave the rest of his life to the development of this community and the propagation in America and England of the ideas which governed it. So the whole Moravian movement received the stamp of his genius. He was a man who called forth intense love from his friends and intense hostility from his critics, and it is easy to account for both. He was generous both in his ideas and in his use of his wealth, single-minded in his devotion to Christ and the ideal of Christian fellowship, warm-hearted and almost magnetic in his relations with his personal friends and supporters. On the other hand his imagination was so vivid as to lead him into embellishments and sometimes perversions of the truth; he was autocratic; he sometimes gave complete rein to his own and other people's emotionalism; his business methods were unpractical and sometimes dubious.

Under Zinzendorf the Herrnhut community sought to recapture the spirit of the practice of first-century Christianity—though their efforts were not always directed by very exact historical knowledge. The sexes were kept strictly apart in the services of worship, and in the day-to-day life of the community the 'Married Choir', the 'Single Brethren', the 'Single Sisters', the widowers, and the children were segregated. They revived the practice of the '*Agape*' as they imagined it to have been: that is, they took a meal of rye bread and water together, and wished each other 'Long live the Lord Jesus in our hearts'. Hymn-singing played a large part in their worship and life: at nine o'clock every morning the young men sang hymns as they marched round the settlement. They had a simple belief in immediate answer to prayer, and in accordance with this, when a difficult decision had to be made, they asked God for guidance, and then drew lots to discover what His guidance was. Twelve Elders, elected by the vote of all the male adults, governed the proceedings of the community. Their services were conducted in the early days of Herrnhut by both ordained ministers and laymen, but the laymen dropped out when David Nitschmann was consecrated bishop by Bishop Daniel Ernst Jablonski and was able to ordain

renunciation is abundantly worth while. 'If a Person was
walk upon a Rope across some great River, and he was bid
deny himself the Pleasure of walking in silver Shoes, or looki
about at the Beauty of the Waves, or listening to the Noise
Sailors, if he was commanded to deny himself the Advantage
fishing by the Way, would there be any Hardship in such Se
Denial?'

It might be thought that these are 'counsels of perfection'
the sense that they are intended only for those who withdr
themselves entirely from the world. But no. Both in this treat
and in the one that followed it in 1728, *A Serious Call to
Devout and Holy Life*, Law makes it very plain that he is n
giving advice to cloistered saints, but instructing ordinary peo
in their ordinary callings. In other words, he applies the couns
of perfection, the plain, explicit commands of the Gospel, a
the Sermon on the Mount in particular, to every man in th
station of life to which it shall please God to call him. *All* 'ord
of people' are to live Christ-like lives, and 'to the utmost of th
power, to make their life agreeable to the one Spirit for who
they all pray'.

No doubt many other writers had said such things before. B
Law succeeds in saying them with so much urgency and pungen
that it is very difficult to read his treatises without many searc
ings of heart and conscience, and without suspecting that t
excuse that the author, after all, knew very little about t
exigencies of practical life, is a lame one.

We noted the early history of the Moravians in the la
chapter. A complete change came over them in the eighteen
century, largely connected with the work and personality
Count Nicolaus Ludwig von Zinzendorf (1700–60). He w
brought up in pietistic circles in Lutheran Saxony, and r
mained loyal to the principles of Lutheran theology, as l
conceived it (and his orthodoxy, though questioned, was nev
condemned), all his life. The ordinary practices of the Sta
Church did not satisfy him, and from quite an early age l
organized 'religious societies' in his own home and elsewher
These were attended chiefly by people of his own noble ran
in life, and he wished to share their blessings with others as we
So he bought an estate, later called Herrnhut, in Saxony, an
welcomed there all those who wished to come, especially refuge
from Austria who belonged to the Church of the Brethren (th

ministers in a properly ordered succession; the office of bishop was, however, purely spiritual.

It would seem that Zinzendorf had no original intention of forming a separate Church, but only of gathering together earnest believers to form an *ecclesiola in ecclesia*. When events compelled the Church of the Brethren to become an independent Episcopal Church (recognized as such by the Church of England in 1749), he was zealous in maintaining cooperation with all denominations in all countries. He thought it the duty of Christians to learn something from every Church—from the Roman Catholics, poverty of spirit and a deep regard for the Church in Paradise; from the Calvinists, the doctrine of that 'election by which the heritage of the Lamb is called out'; from the Lutherans, the universal mercy of God and the true consolation which comes from the Sacrament; from the Quakers, freedom for every individual conscience; and from the Mennonites, strict standards of Christian moral life.* In 1741 he went to Pennsylvania, and found that the various Churches were competing with each other in the evangelization of the Indians. He persuaded them all to come together in several Synods, and to consider forming themselves into 'the Congregation of God in the Spirit', while retaining their denominational loyalties. This great scheme failed in the end—it was too far ahead of its time.

It is easy to recognize the revivified Moravians as Methodists in the sense defined in the last chapter. One of their consuming passions was the evangelization of the heathen; and it was in the pursuit of this aim that some of them met John Wesley, and changed the direction of his spiritual career.

* M. Schmidt in *A History of the Ecumenical Movement*, ed. by R. Rouse and S. C. Neill, pp 101 ff. (cf. pp 229 ff., D. H. Yoder).

CHAPTER THREE

John and Charles Wesley

The Wesley family might have attained a modest eminence in the annals of the eighteenth century even if two of its members had not begun a national religious movement. The head of the family was the Reverend Samuel Wesley, Rector of Epworth in Lincolnshire from 1697 until his death in 1735. Epworth was then a remote and not very attractive village, surrounded for much of the year by the waters of the North Lincolnshire marshlands. The living was poorly endowed, and the parishioners boorish and notably unwilling to pay their tithes. Samuel was a faithful but not very successful pastor. He was a learned man, and a would-be poet and theologian, whose *maximum opus* was a protracted commentary on the Book of Job, published shortly before his death, and rarely read since (its binding was much admired by Queen Caroline, to whom it was dedicated). His father was a Dissenting minister ejected in 1662, but he himself was a convinced Churchman of strong Tory principles. In fact, his principles were certainly the strongest thing about him, and made him exceedingly obstinate. He was rash in the expression of his opinions, and incompetent in the management of his finances. The former defect brought upon him the occasional violence of his flock, and the latter landed him in Lincoln Castle for a year. The deed for which it is hardest for a modern Christian to forgive him is his treatment of his daughter Hetty when she disgraced herself;* but this also sprang from his unyielding principles. Methodist historians have tried hard to whitewash their hero's father, but not with any great success. He was, however, affectionate in a blundering way, and his son John loved and respected him.

The most sensible thing he ever did was to marry Susanna

* She was engaged to a lawyer, who seduced her; her father married her off to a worthless fellow called Wright, a plumber. The story is movingly told in A. Quiller-Couch's *Hetty Wesley*.

Annesley. Her father, Dr Samuel, was a notable Dissenting minister,* but she renounced Dissenting principles at the age of thirteen, though they never ceased to flow in her blood. Her principles were as strong as her husband's, and sometimes in conflict with them; but she had the saving graces of imagination and willingness to learn, and she knew how to temper principle with compassion. She was clear-headed and independent, and no mean student of theology. While her husband was detained in Lincoln Castle she conducted services for the parish in the rectory kitchen, and spiritedly defended the practice when her husband returned. But at the base of her character was her personal religion. Her own words give some idea of this:

> For me to know our Lord only as a man is to learn that I have done, and daily do, many things contrary to Thy divine nature and the dictates of my own reason, which must necessarily lead me to despair. But to behold Thee in Jesus Christ, reconciling the world unto Thyself: by faith to see Thee, the infinite, all glorious Being, assuming the character of a Saviour, a repairer of the lapses and healer of the diseases and miseries of mankind, penetrates and melts my soul. It is something my heart feels and labours under, but my tongue cannot express. I adore Thee, O God! I adore!

Susanna had borne her husband fourteen children before John was thought of, and the family nearly stopped at that point. For she refused to say 'Amen' at family prayers when Samuel prayed for King William III, and the rector went off to London in a huff, declaring 'if we are to have two kings, we must have two beds'. William III died, however, not many months later, and the accession of Anne, together with an outbreak of fire at the Rectory, made Samuel ready for a reconciliation; the fruit of the reconciliation was John, born on 28 June 1703.† Of the older children, not many survived infancy, and only Samuel, the first-born, and later headmaster of Blundell's School, Tiverton, achieved any prominence. But Hetty (more properly Mehetabel) had a lively and scholarly mind, and Molly (Mary), whose back was deformed, was a person of exceptional grace and kindness. Charles, last but one of the nineteen who made up the eventual total, was born in 1707.

* He was also Daniel Defoe's schoolmaster.

† It has sometimes been stated that Susanna had him christened John Benjamin, perhaps in the hope that he would really be her last offspring. But the baptismal registers of Epworth do not bear this out.

Susanna was certainly the principal factor in the upbringing of both John and Charles. Her husband remained very much in the background, for reasons of both temperament and circumstance. Susanna's methods were, by modern standards, unduly severe: she was not averse from the use of the rod as a means of discipline, the children were to be seen and not heard at mealtimes, and even the babies were not allowed to cry, except very softly. Formal education began when the age of five was reached, and lasted for six hours a day from the start. John responded very favourably to this treatment, and there is no record that the others failed to do the same. Certainly they all mastered foreign languages at an early age, and retained a taste for them throughout life. When John Wesley came to found schools of his own, he looked back to the educational principles and practice of his mother for guidance.

One of Susanna Wesley's achievements was to bind her family into a very closely-knit unit. She was helped in this by the fact that the Wesley family was forced by its geographical isolation in the Lincolnshire fens to be socially and culturally self-supporting. But this by itself might have led to endless frictions within the family. Because of Susanna's noble integrity and all-encompassing love exactly the opposite took place. Yet it is probable that she watched over John with an extra amount of loving care and attended to his education with special diligence, because of an event in his childhood to which she attached the highest significance.

The vestries of Methodist chapels in the nineteenth century were frequently bedizened with one or other of three specimens of Methodist Victorian art, each depicting a favourite object of Methodist reminiscence. One showed Wesley's deathbed, one the Holy Club in Oxford, and one (by far the most exciting) the great fire of Epworth Rectory when John was five years old. It was this last event which influenced Susanna so much. It may have been caused by the active ill-will of the parishioners, but it should be said in their defence that a building such as the Rectory could well have been ignited by something much less sinister. John, in the nursery at the top, was cut off by the flames; but with singular presence of mind he pushed a chest to the window, stood on it, and indicated his whereabouts to the rescuers below. So he came to safety. This was to the bystanders, and especially to his mother, an evident sign of God's especial interest in the boy. To her, and indeed to himself, he was for ever afterwards 'a brand plucked from the burning' in both the literal and the metaphorical sense.

At the age of ten and a half John went to the Charterhouse, then, of course, still in London. We know very little of his career at the school, except that he was quick and proficient at his studies and maintained his interest in religion and religious practices in what may not have been a very favourable environment. In the holidays he lodged with his elder brother Samuel, now an usher at Westminster School. After six years he obtained an Exhibition to Christ Church, Oxford, and went up in the autumn of 1720.

At Oxford there was little incentive either to learning or to religion. The inability of the senior university of this country to provide in the eighteenth century 'a succession of fit persons to serve in Church and State' must be put down partly to the fact that it was a nest of Non-Jurors and Jacobites, none of whom had any strong desire to serve either Church or State as they were then constituted. Nor was the Government eager to give preferment to men who came from such a place. But there was also a deeper reason: the things of the mind and spirit had come to be of little account among both teachers and students, even those who fulfilled their obligations with some degree of conscientiousness. Lest the strictures of religious critics be thought to be biased, it is enough to quote the familiar words of Edward Gibbon on the subject of the dons of his College: 'Easy men who supinely enjoyed the gifts of the founder. . . . Their conversation stagnated in a round of College business, Tory politics, personal anecdotes of scandal; their dull and deep potations excused the brisk intemperance of youth.' And they were virtually all clergymen.

John Wesley, during his first five years at the University, kept himself free, of course, from the grosser sins of his contemporaries. (We say 'of course', because it is difficult to think of him as giving way to sensuality.) He worked much harder than most of his fellow-students, and made much more progress; he continued to perform his religious duties, though he tells us that this was out of sheer habit. In a word, nothing took place that is of much importance in the history either of Methodism or of John Wesley's soul. But it was in these years, no doubt, that he came (as he said in later years) to 'love the very sight of Oxford'—like all her true sons.

In September 1725 he was ordained deacon by the Bishop of Oxford. Probably the decision to ask for ordination was not in itself a very momentous one. It must have been expected from the start that a man of his tastes, education, antecedents, and temperament would eventually be ordained, and John Wesley shared and in due course fulfilled the general expectation. But the year 1725 was marked for him by a fresh application of his mind to works of Christian devotion, and it seems natural to suppose that it was the thought of his ordination that impelled him in this direction. The first books that captured his attention were Jeremy Taylor's *Holy Living* and *Holy Dying*; these gave him a 'fixed intention to give himself up to God'. Then he turned to à Kempis's *Imitation of Christ*, and 'longed to give God all his heart'. He came across William Law's *Christian Perfection* and *A Serious Call* very soon after they were published in 1726 and 1729, and these had a more profound effect on him than anything that he had ever read before outside the Bible:

> But meeting now with Mr Law's *Christian Perfection* and *Serious Call,* although I was much offended at many parts of both, yet they convinced me more than ever of the exceeding height and breadth and depth of the law of God. The light flowed in so mightily upon my soul, that everything appeared in a new view. I cried to God for help, and resolved not to prolong the time of obeying him as I had never done before. And by my continued endeavour to keep His whole law, inward and outward, to the utmost of my power, I was persuaded that I should be accepted of Him, and that I was even then in a state of salvation.

This far-reaching resolution on Wesley's part is sometimes called his 'first conversion', and those who think that an undue emphasis has been placed in some quarters on his 'evangelical conversion' in 1738 are inclined to suggest that this was his *real* conversion. Neither of these terms seems to fit the situation, but this is not to deny that the period following his ordination gave a new aim to his life. What seems to have happened is that now for the first time he became really aware of the necessity for 'holiness' if a man is to be in the favour of God—for 'without holiness no man shall see the Lord'—and strove thereafter with might and main to achieve it; hence the extreme austerity of his life, hence his regular attendance at the 'means of grace', hence his unremitting works of charity, hence his ceaseless desire to preach the Gospel to the godless and the heathen. All this was the quest for Christian Perfection, which he now knew it was the duty of all real Christians to undertake. But it was a conflict as well as a quest, and for fourteen years, for all his good works and religious exercises and scrutiny of his soul—no one was ever more ready than he to pluck up his soul by the roots and examine its growth—he seemed to himself to come no nearer the goal for which he had set out. He was a Christian all his life, and from 1725 he was a zealous and earnest Christian, but he was not a Christian at peace with God and with himself.

But religion by no means took up all his time and energy. In March 1726 he was elected a Fellow of Lincoln College, not without some assiduous canvassing of influential friends by his father. It seems that Lincoln was relatively free from the prevailing idleness and corruption, and Wesley soon found himself lecturing on Greek and philosophy, presiding over the daily disputations on logical subjects still surviving in Oxford from the Middle Ages, and giving private instruction to his pupils. There was time for some social activity, too. From time to time he rode forty miles to the Rectory at Stanton in the Cotswolds, to be hospitably entertained by Robert, Sally, and Betty Kirkham; and perhaps for a time he was a little in love with Sally. Nor had he any objection to playing cards, drinking wine, and visiting the theatre with his friends.*

He was often accompanied on these trips by his brother Charles, who came up to Christ Church in 1726. The two brothers also, in spite of Charles's declared intention not to 'be made a saint all at once', began the practice of reading together in each other's rooms both classical literature and books on divinity, adding to John's favourites, à Kempis, Taylor, and Law, such works as those of John Norris of Bemerton on personal religion and Henry Scougal's *Life of God in the Soul of Man*. But these studious delights had soon to be abandoned by John, for in the summer of 1727 his father, finding the duties of his parish growing more irksome than ever, asked his son to come and help him. John came, and for two years acted as his father's curate in the village of Wroote, not very far from Epworth, but divided from it by unpleasant marshland, and itself a dirty and

* The best description of his academic and social life during his Oxford days is to be found in V. H. H. Green, *The Young Mr Wesley* (1961).

untidy hamlet. It cannot have been with unmixed sorrow that he received a letter from the Rector of Lincoln summoning him to return to his Oxford responsibilities. He had been back for a short time to be ordained priest in 1728, and on one or two other occasions. Now he may well have felt that he was returning for good, with marriage and the consequent removal to a parochial cure of souls as the only possible—and not very likely—alternative.

Back in Oxford he found that Charles had gathered round him a group of friends to read and pray regularly together. They had formed the resolve, startling in those days, to keep strictly to the statutes of the University, and proceeded to organize themselves on the lines of a Religious Society. They pledged themselves to be regular in their private devotions, and in particular to take the Sacrament of Holy Communion once a week; to attend carefully to their ethical and religious conduct; to meet together each evening from six to nine o'clock to read, study, and discuss the Bible and other books of sacred learning; and to visit both the town and the University prisons once or twice a week. John was invited to join in the proceedings, and very soon, partly because he was the only ordained member of the group, and senior to the others in the University, partly because of his obvious and natural gifts, he was the acknowledged leader.

It cannot be too strongly stressed that this was not Methodism as it later emerged in the life of England, though it was no doubt the ground out of which Methodism grew. It is true that the name is the same; various sobriquets were attached to the group by derisive undergraduates when its activities became known—such as 'The Enthusiasts', 'The Bible Moths', 'The Holy Club'—but the one which stuck was 'The Methodists' (presumably given because of the curiously methodical way of life which they followed). It is true that Wesley took over some of the habits and customs of the group into Methodism proper. It is true also that the aim of the group was personal holiness, as it was of the later Methodist Societies. But the ideal of holiness suffered a sea-change, as we shall see, before it became the chief aim of Wesley's evangelical work: the members of the 'Holy Club' looked inward to their souls, and not outward to the needy world, except in so far as it provided suitable objects of their charity; very few of them continued with Wesley into the next stage of his development, and when he set out to convert England, Wesley himself was a very different man from the prim and donnish clergyman who hurried to and from his devotions through the streets of Oxford. The Oxford 'Methodists' were a company of rather priggish young men who were horrified by the things they saw around them and were determined to save their own souls in the only way they knew.

This comes out very clearly in the answer which John sent to his father's request to apply for the living of Epworth on his impending retirement through old age. The answer ran into twenty-six paragraphs, but the nub of it lies in these words:

> My one aim in life is to secure personal holiness, for without being holy myself I cannot promote real holiness in others. In Oxford, conversing only with a chosen circle of friends, I am screened from all the frivolous importunities of the world, and here I have a better chance of becoming holy than I should have in any other place. . . . I should be of no use at all: I could not do any good to those boorish people, and I should probably fall beck into habits of irregularity and indulgence.

There is here, of course, the adumbration of a desire to help others on the path which he had himself adopted; and he goes on in another passage to say:

> Here are poor to be relieved, children to be educated, workhouses and prisons to be visited; and lastly, here are the schools of the prophets, here are tender minds to be formed and strengthened.

But the desire for personal holiness occupies the centre of the picture.

This is not to say, however, that Wesley learned nothing from the 'Holy Club' and its members. On the contrary, the sacrificial philanthropy of William Morgan made a permanent impression upon him; and John Clayton, a non-juror and a keen sacramentalist, persuaded him to vow to baptize by immersion, to use the oblation of the elements and the invocation of the Holy Spirit in the Eucharist, to pray for the faithful departed, to observe Lent, and to turn to the east at the Creed.

University societies tend to rise and fall, according to the enthusiasm of the members, the efficiency of the officers, and the claims of examinations; many of them have their day and cease to be. In the natural course of events, the members of the 'Holy Club' went down from Oxford one by one, and by

1735 less than half a dozen were left, including John and Charles Wesley. It was at this point, when in any case John was probably looking round for new fields of useful enterprise, that the impressive personality of General James Edward Oglethorpe made itself known to him. Oglethorpe was a truly remarkable man, remarkable for military daring (he was made A.D.C. to Prince Eugene by the Duke of Marlborough on this score), for his large designs for the welfare of his fellow men, and for his highly successful blend of patriotism and philanthropy. Returning home at the end of his military career, he was very much distressed by the state of the debtors' prisons and those who inhabited them; the extreme folly of consigning to prison a man (with his family) because he could not pay his debts, keeping him there until he paid them, and thus robbing him of the chance of ever paying them, had not so far occurred to anyone. Oglethorpe persuaded the House of Commons to carry out some reforms of the system, and then had the even better idea of giving the debtors the opportunity to make good in the New World. In 1732, by royal charter, he founded the colony of Georgia. Here he made friends with the Indians, and brought back one of their chiefs, Tomo-Chichi, as an advertisement for the colony. This was a highly successful device, for Tomo-Chichi soon became the toast of the London *salons*, and induced many others, as well as defaulting debtors, to go out to Georgia. Neither the Government nor Oglethorpe were unaware of a further advantage of the scheme, that the Spanish were advancing into the territory from Florida in the south, and the colony would form an effective bastion against them.

Oglethorpe was sincerely concerned for the spiritual as well as the physical welfare of the colonists, and when he met the Wesley brothers he was quite sure that in them he had very effective agents for this. He invited John to be the pastor of the English community in Savannah, the capital of the colony, with a half-implied promise that he would have the chance of preaching to the Indians; and he invited Charles to be his personal secretary. They were not eager to leave their recently-bereaved mother, but Susanna said firmly that if she had twenty sons she would want them all to be missionaries in Georgia, and John was entranced by a highly romantic vision of the 'noble savage' which he had gained from current literature (it was not borne out by the reality).

Oglethorpe, John and Charles Wesley, and their friends Charles Delamotte and Benjamin Ingham, were on board the good ship *Simmonds* from 21 October 1735 to 6 February 1736, but they did not begin their voyage over the Atlantic until some days after 10 December, when they finally sailed out of Cowes Roads. During the calm days at the beginning, the Wesleys and their friends quickly put in hand their chaplaincy duties, holding services and Bible readings, celebrating the Sacrament, and instructing the children, with great regularity. But the Atlantic storms began to interrupt the proceedings, and made John Wesley (as he shamefacedly admitted to himself) more anxious for his own skin than for the souls of his fellow-travellers. There was a party of twenty-six Germans on board, whose language John learned with the express purpose of being able to converse with them. They were Moravians, seeking a new home in America as a haven from their hardships in Central Europe. When everyone else on the ship was terrified by the storms, the Moravians were quite unperturbed; when the mainmast was split into pieces and the English screamed in panic, they went on singing hymns. Wesley was vastly impressed, as well he might be, and when the storm was over asked them whether their women and children had not been afraid. 'No,' one of them gently replied. 'Our women and children are not afraid to die.'

The party landed in Georgia on an island of the Savannah river. The country around is nowadays extensively developed, with luxury hotels, golf courses, and bathing beaches; but its climate is bleak in winter and sultry and stormy in summer, and it must have looked very desolate to Wesley when he first arrived. But he was cheered by the sight of pine groves, which showed 'the bloom of spring in the depth of winter', and nerved to the work ahead of him by the arrival of August Gottlieb Spangenberg, pastor of the Moravians already in the colony, who had come to welcome his co-religionists. Remembering the God-given courage of the Moravians on the ship, he asked the pastor for advice about his future conduct.

Spangenberg said to him rather abruptly: 'Have you the witness within yourself? Does the Spirit of God bear witness with your spirit that you are a child of God?' Wesley did not know what to answer, and Spangenberg pressed him further: 'Do you know Jesus Christ?'

Wesley replied: 'I know He is the Saviour of the world.'

'True. But do you know He has saved you?'

Wesley answered: 'I hope He has died to save me.'

Spangenberg was not even yet satisfied: 'Do you know yourself?' he asked.

Wesley replied: 'I do.' But he adds in his *Journal*: 'I fear they were vain words.'

Fortunately for our desire to know Wesley's spiritual state at that time, the journal of Spangenberg himself has been recently discovered; it records the same discussion, and adds by way of comment: 'I noticed that true grace dwelt and reigned in him.'

In this short conversation we hear two notes of Wesley's later preaching—the inward witness of the Spirit (which his father, as it happened, had stressed a few months before in his last words to his son), and the knowledge of *personal* salvation through Christ. Clearly the simple words of Spangenberg had a great effect on John at this point in his development.

John's main duties were in Savannah, with occasional visits to Frederica, the garrison town on the coast; Charles seems to have spent almost all his time in Frederica. In both places the brothers and their friends made the same mistake. They tried to turn the community into a Holy Club, with full accompaniment of sacramental observances. But though its members were in some cases respectable people, in many cases they were the rag-tag and bobtail of the London debtor-prisons, and the Wesleys treated them all as if they were pious undergraduates. The failure was more complete in Frederica than in Savannah, perhaps because Charles was even less able to cope with difficult people than John was. His two principal *bêtes noires* were two dubiously moral and undoubtedly scurrilous women called Mrs Hawkins and Mrs Welch, who had no hesitation in claiming, first, that they had committed adultery with Oglethorpe, and secondly that Charles Wesley had disseminated this abominable lie. Neither John nor Charles had yet enough knowledge of the evil in the human heart to deal with this sort of thing.

The crisis of failure was precipitated by a delightful and apparently religious young woman by the name of Sophia Hopkey, niece of Mr Causton, chief magistrate of Savannah. John was attracted by her, and she was attracted by his position in society. She was certainly willing to marry him, and he wanted to marry her; but he was greatly troubled by the implications of marriage for his manner of life and his pastoral office. He hesitated, and finally asked for the advice of the Moravians, who told him to put the marriage out of his head. Even then he wavered slightly, and when he heard that Sophy, tired of waiting for the decisive word, had agreed to marry a Mr Williamson, he knew what his real wishes had been. But it was too late. After her marriage Sophy showed herself to be what she really was, an ordinary and fairly gay young woman. Shocked by her behaviour, Wesley very unwisely, and perhaps with unconscious vindictiveness, repelled her from Communion. An action for defamation of character was brought against him, but before it came to a conclusion Wesley had sailed for home—and perhaps this was his enemies' object in bringing the action. Charles had already left America, in despair at his lack of success.

So the brothers had apparently wasted two years of their life. But had they? They had gained a knowledge of themselves which could never have come to them in the seclusion of Oxford or a country parish. So it was not all loss. But John had never preached to the Indians at all, and from a purely practical point of view all that remained to show for the Georgian experience was a volume of Moravian hymns translated from the German with great vigour by John Wesley, one of them in its content sadly contrary to John's actual condition:

> Now I have found the ground wherein
> Sure my soul's anchor may remain.

The next few months were agonizing ones for both John and Charles. John had followed the path of 'inward and outward holiness' for fourteen years, and he had arrived nowhere. He wrote in his *Journal* on his return to England:

> It is now two years and almost four months since I left my native country, in order to teach the Georgian Indians the nature of Christianity: but what have I learned myself in the meantime? Why (what I least of all suspected), that I who went to America to convert others, was never myself converted to God.

This was exaggerated self-condemnation, and in later years John himself added a footnote to this entry in the *Journal*: 'I am not sure of this.' But the fact remained that for all his pursuit of holiness he now knew himself to lack control of his inward feelings, and to have what he himself calls 'a fair summer religion'. Above all, he was not at peace with God; he was trying to 'establish his own righteousness', as he put it, and all the good deeds that he was able to amass still left him with the sense of condemnation in the eyes of a righteous God.

In this predicament he met Peter Böhler, a Moravian staying in England for a few weeks before going on to America. Because of his past experience with the Moravians, he was very willing to hear what Böhler had to say, and spent as much time as possible with him. Böhler was a man of simple and direct religious outlook, and felt the complexities of Wesley's theological reasoning to be serious hindrances to genuine Christianity. 'My brother, my brother, that philosophy of yours must be purged away,' he urged, much to John's puzzlement and chagrin. But John was sure that Böhler could help him when no one else could, and began to see that the real drift of his advice was that he lacked 'the faith whereby alone we are saved'. In other words, all his mighty efforts after holiness had been ineffectual because he lacked the foundation of it all—simple, personal trust in Jesus Christ his Saviour. That was why his religion had been a burden and not a delight, that was why he was under the law, and not under grace'. By the beginning of March 1738, just over a month since landing in England, he 'was clearly convinced of unbelief', and concluded that he ought to stop preaching. 'No,' said Böhler. 'Preach faith till you have it; and then, because you have it, you will preach faith.' This paradoxical advice was effective. The struggle for faith continued, and at the beginning of May, Böhler left for America. But on 24 May—as every Methodist the world over is reminded every year—peace was granted.

The main events of that day, the day of what may properly be called John Wesley's 'evangelical conversion', are worth briefly recording. At 5 a.m., according to his ascetic habit, he opened his Greek Testament, and this time he lighted on the words in II Peter: 'there are given to us exceeding great and precious promises, even that ye should be partakers of the divine nature.' Some time during the day he wrote in the following terms to a friend:

> I see that God's law is holy, righteous, and good. I know that every thought, every movement of my heart should bear God's image. But how deep I have fallen! How far I am from God's glory! I feel that I am sold under sin. I know that I deserve only wrath. . . . God is holy. I am sinful. God is a consuming fire; it must devour me the sinner.

He heard the anthem at evensong at St Paul's: 'Out of the depths have I cried unto Thee.' The rest must be told in his own words:

In the evening I went very unwillingly to a society in Aldersgate Street, where one was reading Luther's preface of the Epistle to the Romans. About a quarter before nine, while he was describing the change which God works in the heart through faith in Christ, I felt my heart strangely warmed. I felt I did trust in Christ, Christ alone, for salvation; and an assurance was given me that He had taken away my sins, even mine, and saved me from the law of sin and death.

'Saving faith' had been given to him, and the assurance of forgiveness. This was the essence of it. When we read that his 'heart was strangely warmed', we are to understand that the conscious emotion which accompanied the great deliverance was strange to him, for he was not an emotional man. We do not know that this 'strange warmth' ever visited him again; his life thereafter was founded, not on an emotion, but on the gift of God granted to him at that moment and continued to him, with occasional interruptions, through all his remaining days.

By coincidence, or Providence, his brother Charles had gone through the same spiritual development, in a lower key perhaps, but no less genuinely; he had submitted himself to the guidance of the same Peter Böhler, and three days before John he had found liberation through the same gift of faith. But he was in bed, recovering from pleurisy, when John came round, late on the evening of 24 May, to tell him what had happened to him. Together the brothers and their friends sang the hymn which Charles had just written to describe his experience:

Where shall my wondering soul begin?
How shall I all to heaven aspire?
A slave redeemed from death and sin,
A brand plucked from eternal fire,
How shall I equal triumphs raise,
Or sing my great Deliverer's praise?

Outcasts of men, to you I call,
Harlots, and publicans, and thieves!
He spreads his arms to embrace you all:
Sinners alone His grace receives:
No need of Him the righteous have;
He came the lost to seek and save.

Psychologically, there is no doubt that this was a complete turning-point in the life of John Wesley. Until now his immense spiritual and mental energies had been mostly directed upon himself; he had spent innumerable hours, not only during the preceding months, but for most of his life, brooding upon the state of his soul and trying to improve it. Now those energies were released, and immediately directed outward to those of his fellow men who stood in need of the same liberation as he had himself received. Personal salvation for himself was no longer his all-absorbing aim. In fact, he virtually forgot it in his enterprise to bring salvation to others. That the same was true of his brother is shown by the fact that in his 'birthday hymn' just quoted he passes straight from his exultation in sins forgiven to the summons to 'harlots, and publicans, and thieves'.

Theologically 24 May 1738 was no less important. John Wesley had accepted from William Law and others the 'serious call' to personal holiness, and obeyed it to the limits of his power. Nor did he ever throughout the whole of his life abate by one jot his demand on all Christians to strive for holiness; he fought tooth and nail against those who claimed that once a man was forgiven by God there was nothing further for him to do, and he strongly condemned Martin Luther for seeming to suggest that this was so (the charge was no doubt unjust). But now, through Böhler, he saw that he had omitted one vital stage on the way to holiness, in fact the very entrance to the way, personal faith in Jesus Christ, without which it is useless to try to be holy. Faith leading to holiness, not holiness by itself, was now his understanding of the Christian life.

Thus he was able to restore two integral parts of the Catholic Faith to the teaching and preaching of the Church of England, faith and holiness, which in his time were receiving merely formal and often meaningless mention. Faith was intellectual assent to rational truth; holiness was practical charity, or as Joseph Butler more clearly put it, 'enlightened self-interest'. Wesley restored the Scriptural sense of both words, and so was able to preach a message much nearer to the wholeness of the Faith than any of his non-Methodist contemporaries. Needless to say, he did not therefore omit any item of the Creeds or of liturgical practice; he was at least as orthodox and catholic as any bishop of his time. How the Church of England reacted to this attempted renewal of its catholicity remains to be told.

There was another theological consequence of the 'conversion', only slightly less important. John Wesley on the date in question was 'assured' that Christ had taken away his sins, even his. This fact soon led him to inquire into the meaning of 'assurance', and to work out its Scriptural basis under the name of 'the witness of the Spirit'. Thus he restored another doctrine of the preaching of the Catholic Faith, a doctrine very much overlaid in Wesley's time, and, it must be confessed, open to easy misunderstanding (as we shall see), both by Wesley's supporters and by his opponents.

We have come to the point at which the personal concerns of the brothers Wesley are about to be taken up into a national ecclesiastical movement. They will appear hereafter rather as leaders and counsellors of their brethren and followers than as individual people. So it is worth while to look for the last time at their personal qualities and particular experiences.

John was a small man, always neat in his clothing and appearance, calm and restrained in manner and expression. But his jaw was firm, and his eyes piercing; when he preached, every member of the congregation felt that the message was directed towards him alone. He was never rattled by an emergency, and hardly ever lost his temper. Once he had found spiritual peace, he had no fear of death; and when a mob was let loose against him, he was invariably the one person in control of the situation and the people involved in it. Leadership and authority, organizing skill and logical statement, came naturally to him.

There was also much of the autocrat in him, and his followers sometimes, ruefully but not inaccurately, referred to him as 'Pope John'. He was not always as consistent as he claimed to be, and cannot be freed from the suspicion of sometimes adjusting his principles to what he had found useful in practice. He took his own advice, 'never be triflingly employed', too literally, and there is justice in Samuel Johnson's complaint: 'John Wesley's conversation is good, but he is never at leisure. He is always obliged to go at a certain hour. This is very disagreeable to a man who loves to fold his legs and have out his talk, as I do.'

In his personal relationships he was quietly courteous and relaxed, and often affectionate. He had no difficulty in getting on with children, or with those who were less intelligent and less virtuous than himself; he spent almost all his time with such people. But with women as women (though not as Christian people) he never came to terms. The unfortunate affair with Sophy Hopkey was repeated later in his life, of course with changes, with Grace Murray, the handsome widow of a sea captain, converted by Wesley's preaching and later put in charge of the Orphan House in Newcastle upon Tyne. She was a brave and zealous woman, sincere in her devotion to God, but impetuous, imperious, and probably a little unstable. Wesley met her when he was forty-five and she was thirty-two. There is little doubt that he fell in love with her as deeply as he was capable of doing. But once again he hesitated—and for a travelling evangelist, who was also the leader of a movement spreading over the whole country and demanding his presence here, there, and everywhere, the decision was bound to be a complex one; and Grace had another suitor, John Bennet, more pressing and less complicated. Charles Wesley had no doubt that Grace was a quite unsuitable mate for his brother, and when John wrote that he contemplated marrying her, he moved more quickly than ever before in his life, from Bristol to Newcastle, to intervene. When he arrived, having picked up Grace on the way, John Wesley was elsewhere. John Bennet was summoned, and married to Grace before John came back. The varying emotions of Grace herself during this exciting period are not recorded, and John Wesley's *Journal* is silent about his.

The unhappiest story of all is that of his actual marriage. Undeterred by the Grace Murray experience, John decided that he ought to marry and proposed to Mrs Vazeille, a merchant's widow of forty-one. She accepted, to the lasting regret of both parties. Mrs Vazeille was to all appearances, and in the knowledge of her friends, a discreet, amiable, and good-hearted woman. After marriage she turned out to be a termagant, permanently jealous of all her husband's friends, and sometimes insanely so. John made matters worse by refusing to curtail his journeyings by a single mile. She tried accompanying him, but found the hardships intolerable. From then on man and wife gradually went apart, and she sometimes pursued him with scurrilous abuse. When she died in 1781 John did not even hear of the event until after the funeral.

There has been much theorizing about John's alleged 'mother-fixation', and consequent inability to make the necessary adjustments for a satisfactory marriage. A simpler explanation is that the personality and character of his mother, which dominated his childhood, gave him a very high view of all women, and caused him to idealize completely those to whom he became attached.

Charles was also a small man, but fuller than John in face and figure. He was extremely sociable by nature, cheerful and sometimes aggressive, but also liable to fits of black depression. No mean scholar, he yet took much more readily to poetic expression than to close reasoning, and was very much more emotional than his brother. He also had a strong vein of obstinacy. He was a successful preacher, and still more effective in administering comfort to people in great distress, not least to criminals condemned to death. But he had not the resilience or energy of John; after a few years of vigorous itinerancy he settled down to domesticity in Bristol, and became the resident pastor of the Methodist people there. There was music as well as poetry in him, and this came out in his brilliant sons, Charles and Samuel, and his even more distinguished grandson, Samuel Sebastian. Charles aroused great affection in his friends, and his brother John remained deeply attached to him, even after his egregious conduct in the matter of Grace Murray.

Charles had no matrimonial difficulties. He married Sarah Gwynne, the daughter of a country squire from Breconshire, in 1749, at the age of forty-two, and they lived happily ever after, except for a grievous attack of smallpox which ruined Sarah's excellent features, and the premature death of several of their children. Sarah was kindly, pious, and patient, showed herself a splendid hostess when the family moved to London in 1771, and gave concerts and decorous parties in their spacious residence in Chesterfield Street, Marylebone.

No one doubts that John was a better and greater man than Charles, but there is a sense in which Charles made it possible for John to carry out his mission, not only by the hymns which he contributed, but by the quality of affectionate yet critical loyalty in which he never failed.

CHAPTER FOUR

The Revival

The originator of the Methodist Revival was neither John nor Charles Wesley, but George Whitefield (1714–70). For a considerable time he was known, at any rate to the public, as its leader, and although his influence steadily decreased, mainly because of his theological differences with John Wesley, it never entirely disappeared, even when his followers were organized separately from those of Wesley. He certainly possessed the most striking personality of the Revival, though his grasp of theological truth and of the principles of Church Order were in a class below Wesley's.

Born in the Bell Inn in Gloucester, he had risen by the age of sixteen to the position of tapster in that hostelry. But his mind was set on a different career, and he managed to find his way as a 'servitor' to Pembroke College, Oxford, at the age of eighteen; Samuel Johnson had left the same college a year before without taking a degree (and also without joining the Holy Club), because of extreme domestic poverty. Whitefield, as a servitor, waited on the other undergraduates and received his education as payment. He soon associated himself with the pious 'Methodists' of the University, and was profoundly influenced by them; at their suggestion he read Scougal's *Life of God in the Soul of Man*, and discovered to his delight and astonishment that 'true religion is a union of the soul with God, or Christ formed within us'. Like the other Oxford Methodists, his chief concern was to live a devout and holy life, and like them he does not seem to have found any particular joy or freedom in doing so. But just before Easter 1735 he underwent an experience which he afterwards described as a 'new birth':

> I was delivered from the burden that had so heavily oppressed me. The spirit of mourning was taken from me, and I knew what it was truly to rejoice in God my Saviour.

The details of this deliverance are not precisely known, but it is certain that it was, in Whitefield's firm belief, instantaneous. It does not seem that the Holy Club particularly encouraged such sudden illuminations, and it may be that Whitefield's 'conversion' had little to do with his membership of it.

But it released a flood of eloquence the like of which has rarely been known in this country. After ordination as deacon, and a brief curacy in an Oxfordshire village, Whitefield decided to go to Oglethorpe's colony in Georgia. But he preached many times in England before departing, partly in order to raise money for the projects which he had in mind for Georgia. His first sermon in Gloucester had been reported to the Bishop as having sent fifteen people mad; the Bishop replied that he hoped they would not recover before the following Sunday. Now in Bristol and other places his preaching had equally striking effects. From 1736 to 1739 he was in America, and the Orphan House which he founded during that time still stands on the road from Brunswick to Savannah. He returned to England to be ordained priest and raise some more money. But he preached everywhere, not for financial reasons alone, but because preaching was in his blood. In Bristol the memory of his previous visit filled the churches so full, when he was billed to preach, that 'some hung upon the rails of the organ-loft, others climbed upon the leads of the church, and altogether made the church so hot with their breath, that the steam would fall from the pillars like drops of rain'. All this, of course, was speedily denounced as '*enthusiasm*', and in any case it reduced the congregations in the churches where Whitefield was not preaching; but before he could be banned from the pulpits he began preaching in the open air, as he had learned to do in America.

In Bristol he heard of the parlous spiritual and physical condition of the colliers of Kingswood Chase, a few miles away, who 'feared not God and regarded not man', and were consequently left severely alone by all human authorities, civil and ecclesiastical, and, to all appearances, by God also. Whitefield decided that he would persuade them that God, at least, cared for them, and acting on what afterwards became one of John Wesley's most treasured maxims, 'Go not to those who want you, but to those who want you most', he went and settled among them. The effect of his preaching on barbarous, simple, and emotional people was spectacular, and they were soon experiencing conversion in large numbers. Whitefield began building a school for their children and organizing them into the elements of civilized life, but saw that he had started something he was not able to complete, for he was due to return to Georgia in the near future. Thinking of his friend John Wesley, and of what he had heard about Wesley's newly found peace of mind, he wrote to ask him to come and help with the work, and continue it when he had to leave the country. Wesley arrived in the spring of 1739.

Whitefield's oratory has often been described, praised, and derided. Its effects are undoubted, and were not limited to the religious sphere; even the acidulated Lord Chesterfield, when Whitefield was narrating in his presence the career of a blind man tottering towards a precipice, suddenly leapt from his chair and shouted: 'By God! He's over!' Probably he owed much to considerable histrionic gifts and an excitingly vivid imagination, and much also, no doubt, to the complete lack of emotional restraint which he often displayed. But he was no mere tear-jerking revivalist, though his opponents tried to make out that he was; he was completely sincere, and his open, generous, tolerant character was wholly consistent with his religious professions.

John Wesley did not accept Whitefield's invitation to Bristol with any great alacrity. Soon after the revolutionary experience of 24 May 1738 he had fulfilled a long-cherished desire to live for a while in Zinzendorf's Moravian settlement at Herrnhut in Saxony. Here he was filled with admiration for the Brethren's zeal and charity, but became uneasy about some elements in the Moravian system. It is hard to be sure just what these were, because the only version which we have of them is perhaps coloured by the conflict which later developed between the Moravians and Wesley. But it may well be that Wesley in Herrnhut began to think that Zinzendorf's position among the Moravians was too autocratic, and that the Moravians as a whole tended to assume that they alone had the true conception of Christianity; certainly he came to think these things not much later.

On his return to England, Wesley accepted and fulfilled all possible invitations to preach with great eagerness, and spent much time with a 'Society' in Fetter Lane in the City of London. This was not a Moravian Society, as has sometimes been thought but a Religious Society of members of the Church of England which was speedily impregnated with Wesley's ideas, especially his new ones on the power of saving faith as the gateway to holiness. It was this Society which really marked the transition from the established Religious Societies of the period to the new type of Society which arose from Wesley's own experience and preaching.

While he was occupied in these comparatively obscure pursuits, Whitefields urgent message came. Wesley was filled with doubts, some returning from the old days of anxious introspection, some springing from his precise and scholarly attitude to truth and its outward expression, some arising from reasonable questions as to the wisdom of unconventional evangelism. For he knew that Whitefield was asking him to preach to barbarians, and he was well aware that the arguments and techniques of a University sermon, or even of a sermon preached in a London parish church, would not meet the case. But this was clearly work which was the logical outcome of his new convictions, and he went.

In Bristol he found what he expected, except that it was probably worse:

> I could scarce reconcile myself to this strange way of preaching in the fields, of which [Whitefield] set me an example on Sunday; having been all my life (till very lately) so tenacious of every point relating to decency and order, that I should have thought the saving of souls almost a sin, if it had not been done in a church.... At four in the afternoon, I submitted to be more vile, proclaimed in the highways the glad tidings of salvation.

This 'field-preaching' became the principal means by which Wesley and his preachers spread the Gospel through the length and breadth of England, and it is easy to think that Wesley took to it naturally and easily, and found himself thereby in his own element. But this is far from the truth. He disliked it at the start, and at the end of his life he still referred to the discomfort and distress which it had always caused him.

Whitefield's highest hopes of Wesley were that he would 'confirm those that were awakened', and no doubt Wesley himself hoped for nothing greater than that. What actually happened must have surprised both of them beyond measure. After a few days, crowds at least as large came to hear the preaching of Wesley as had assembled for Whitefield; and the effect of the preaching was much more striking. It is customary in all descriptions of Wesley's preaching to draw attention to the unusual psychological phenomena which attended it, and these must be faithfully recorded. Wesley himself described them in great detail in his *Journal*:

Thence I went to Baldwin Street and expounded, as it came in course, the fourth chapter of the Acts. We then called upon God to confirm His word. Immediately one that stood by (to our no small surprise) cried out aloud, with the utmost vehemence, even as in the agonies of death. But we continued in prayer till 'a new song was put in her mouth, a thanksgiving unto our God'. Soon after, two persons (well known in this place, as labouring to live in all good conscience towards all men) were seized with strong pain, and constrained to 'roar for the disquietness of their heart'. But it was not long before they likewise burst forth into praise to God their Saviour.

Again:

A young man was suddenly seized with a violent trembling all over, and in a few minutes, the sorrows of his heart being enlarged, sunk down to the ground. But we ceased not calling upon God, till He raised him up full of 'peace and joy in the Holy Ghost'.

Then again, when Wesley preached to the women in Newgate Gaol in Bristol:

I was insensibly led to declare strongly and explicitly that God 'willeth all men to be saved'; and to pray that 'if this were not the truth of God, He would not suffer the blind to go out of the way; but, if it were, He would bear witness to His word'. Immediately one, and another, and another sunk to the earth; they dropped on every side as thunderstruck. One of them cried aloud. We besought God in her behalf, and he turned her heaviness into joy. A second being in the same agony, we called upon God for her also; and He spoke peace unto her soul.

These strange events were often repeated during the first few years of Wesley's mission; there is even a case of a man who was similarly afflicted, and then relieved, by *reading* one of Wesley's sermons. The pattern seems to have been much the same in most cases. The hearer became distressed ('cut to the heart', as Wesley puts it) by the realization of what sort of person he was (not specifically by the fear of hell, for Wesley's preaching laid no special emphasis on that, though he has often been charged with threatening hell-fire in and out of season); distress turned to despair, which expressed itself physically in trembling and shrieking, and then in sinking unconscious to the ground. Meanwhile Wesley and his friends prayed urgently for the afflicted one's release from torment, and usually peace and sober joy supervened as suddenly as the disturbance had arisen.

Wesley certainly thought at first that these happenings were the work of God, sent, as he says, to 'confirm His word'. They became steadily rarer after the first extravagances, rarer, that is, when the Revival was rapidly gaining ground and was arousing expectation and excitement wherever Wesley went. He could not fail to notice this; he also observed that it was possible to counterfeit the emotions thus expressed. A man of his century could hardly be expected to reach a purely naturalistic explanation, especially when the after-effects of the convulsions were for the most part entirely good—immediate peace of mind, and afterwards an evident change of character. He therefore conceived the theory that the tremblings and agony were the work of Satan, making his last efforts to retain his victim, and that the ensuing peace indicated God's victory over the Adversary. After pondering the matter for many years he definitely rejected the view that they were necessary accompaniments of the work of grace; he admitted that the Devil sometimes had a hand in them; but claimed that 'God suddenly and strongly convinced many; . . . the natural consequences whereof were sudden outcries and strong bodily convulsions'.

Modern psychological man is bound to look at such things in a different light. He will at once think of exhibitionism, mass hysteria, and other states with even more sinister names than these. Their presence, in a highly infectious form, cannot be denied. But it has to be noted that Wesley's words were working on highly suggestible but not necessarily neurotic people; he was saying things of tremendous import that they had never heard before, for their authorized pastors had neglected to teach them, and they were bound to be struck violently, both with dismay and with joy, as they thought first of their sins and then of God's incredible grace and mercy; and many, perhaps very many. of those who went through these shattering experiences continued for the rest of their lives in quiet and practical goodness. It may be that for them a sudden shock was the only, or the best, or at least a harmless way of appropriating divine truth. And it should be remembered that the vast majority of Wesley's converts over the years, and perhaps even in Bristol in the early years, never went through such experiences at all.

But, in any case, much more important than the experiences was the 'after-care' of the converted. Whitefield's preaching had led to the foundation, before Wesley's arrival, of Religious

Societies in Kingswood and Bristol. These were speedily enlarged and increased in number by Wesley. At the very start they received—partly from Whitefield, but much more from Wesley—the character which came to be regarded as distinctively Methodist. The adjective most used for describing this is 'experimental', but this is not sufficiently explicit for modern ears. It was the practice of Wesley to expound a passage of Scripture whenever he visited a Society, and he did so in personal terms, that is, he applied the message directly to those whom he saw before him; prayer was offered in the same personal manner, that those who were present might receive the benefits of salvation, be cured of their illnesses, and be helped in time of temptation. Hymns were sung of which the purport was often equally personal—the first personal pronoun, singular and plural, is very conspicuous in the hymns of the Revival. In other words, the whole emphasis was on a religion which was to be personally accepted, and on an experience of God's forgiveness and power and presence which was to be consciously enjoyed. And the only condition of membership of the Societies was 'the desire to flee from the wrath to come'. It goes without saying that members of the Society were expected to attend on every Sunday the ministrations of their parish clergyman and to take part in the more objective and dignified liturgy of the Established Church.

The Bristol Societies met at first in private houses, but the growth of two of them quickly made it necessary to find a building of their own. Under Wesley's guidance they united to acquire a piece of land in the Horsefair and build a 'Society Room'. Wesley himself undertook to find the money, and in 1741 'the New Room in the Horsefair' was opened. It was at first meant to be simply a place for the Societies to meet; but it became a preaching place also, where men and women not yet members of the Society forgathered to hear the sermons. It was seen to be inadequate for the purposes for which it was being and could be used, and a few years later was rebuilt. Equipped with a room leading off from the chapel below and a Common Room above, and with smaller rooms as bedchambers for itinerant preachers (with one of them especially set apart for Wesley's own use whenever he was in Bristol), it became Wesley's headquarters for the whole of his work in the West of England. The New Room still stands today, in unadorned beauty, right at the heart of Bristol's towering new shopping centre.

When the rebuilding of the New Room was under discussion, it was clearly necessary for effective means of raising money to be discovered; the Methodists were for the most part poor people. A certain Captain Foy earned his right to immortality by the simple suggestion that the members of the Society should be divided into groups of eleven under a leader who should collect a penny a week from each of the eleven. The suggestion was adopted, and it soon became the custom for the 'classes', as they were called, to meet weekly, not only for the payment of 'class money'—though this was continued after the New Room was built, and became a Methodist institution—but also for prayer, Bible Study, and religious conversation. This is the origin of the Methodist Society Class, which became the unit of Society membership, the training ground of lay leaders, and a potent instrument of evangelism. There is no doubt that the 'cellular' organization of the Methodist movement was almost its greatest strength, and not only other religious movements, but also the Trades Unions, the Chartists, the Labour Movement, and to some extent the Communist Party, have paid it the compliment of imitating it. What happened in the Class Meetings must have varied from place to place, time to time, and leader to leader; but the leader was normally a layman—that is, he was neither an ordained clergyman nor a Methodist itinerant preacher—and very often of humble origin and little or no education; the same applied to the members of his Class for the most part, although it was by no means unknown for an employer to be in the Class led by one of his employees. Prayer at the meetings was certainly extemporaneous, and not limited to the leader; the conversation concerned personal matters, and included confession of sins as well as testimony to the power of God. Members absent through sickness or old age were regularly visited by the leader and others, and, if necessary, financially supported; and those absent for other reasons were pleaded with to resume their attendance. Classes for women were separate from those of men, and for this reason women Class Leaders played an important part from the start.

It is hard to believe, but it is certainly the case, that even this type of fellowship was not sufficiently intimate for all of Wesley's purposes. Membership of Class, and therefore of the Methodist Society, required, as we have seen, simply 'the desire to flee from the wrath to come' (which might be thought to be an almost universal desire); but those who had experienced the New Birth and were advancing towards Christian Perfection (and in Wesley's mind, to be regenerate implied at once the obligation to go on to perfection) were gathered into 'bands', smaller groups, also led by laymen, in which the higher reaches of the Christian life could be explored. What was said 'in band' was held to be completely secret and unrepeatable; and even today when Methodists wish to say something highly confidential to each other they sometimes describe themselves as being 'in band'. How far this further elaboration of the Methodist system was actually carried out in Methodism as it spread far and wide is a matter of conjecture, but it was certainly part of Wesley's original intention.

The ground plan of all this organization was laid down by Wesley, after Whitefield's departure, in a series of visits to Bristol, some of them of several months' duration, between 1739 and 1742. His activities did not escape opposition. Sometimes it was of a trivial kind, but one example of this provides us with Wesley's own dry narrative of his encounter with the 'King of Bath', Beau Nash. Wesley, on a visit to Bath, was addressing a large audience—including 'many of the rich and great'—.

> . . . when their champion appeared, and coming close to me, asked by what authority I did these things. I replied: 'By the authority of Jesus Christ, conveyed to me by the (now) Archbishop of Canterbury, when he laid hands upon me, and said *Take thou authority to preach the Gospel!*.' He said: 'This is contrary to Act of Parliament. This is a conventicle.' I answered: 'Sir, the conventicles mentioned in that Act (as the preamble shows) are seditious meetings; but this is not such; here is no shadow of sedition; therefore it is not contrary to that Act.' He replied: 'I say it is; and besides your preaching frightens people out of their wits.' 'Sir, did you ever hear me preach?' 'No.' 'How then can you judge of what you have never heard?' 'Sir, by common report.' 'Common report is not enough. Give me leave, sir, to ask, is not your name Nash?' 'My name is Nash.' 'Sir, I dare not judge you by common report: I think it is not enough to judge by.' Here he paused awhile, and having recovered himself, said: 'I desire to know what this people comes here for.' On which one replied: 'Sir, leave him to me; let an old woman answer him. You, Mr Nash, take care of your body; we take care of our souls; and for the food of our souls we come here.' He replied not a word, but walked away.

More serious was the weighty reproof of the Bishop of Bristol, Joseph Butler, who, as we have seen, was watching over his diocese with much more than the usual episcopal care, and had no doubt received complaints about Wesley's conduct from his clergy. The Bishop summoned him to the Palace. 'Sir,' he said, 'the pretending to extraordinary revelations and gifts of the Holy Spirit is a horrid thing; yes, sir, it is a very horrid thing. . . . You have no business here; you are not commissioned to preach in this diocese: therefore I advise you to go hence.' Wesley refused to obey, and told the Bishop: 'My business on earth is to do what good I can; wherever, therefore, I think I can do most good, there must I stay so long as I think so; at present I think I can do most good here, therefore here I stay.'

The conversation between the two men perfectly expresses the issue that was at stake between them. From Butler's point of view, Wesley was an '*enthusiast*'; and although he was quite wrong in charging him with claiming 'extraordinary revelations', he was right in thinking that Wesley's activities could not be contained within the confines of the Church of England as it then was; they were subversive of diocesan and parochial discipline. Moreover they were surely quite unnecessary. The ordinary services of the Church, properly conducted, and the ordinary ministry of the clergy, properly carried out, were the divinely ordained sufficient means of caring for the souls of Englishmen. But Wesley knew himself to be divinely called, not to contradict or obstruct the work of the bishops and clergy, but rather to help them by supplying what they lacked in doctrine and discipline, and a divine call like that did not brook denial. Legally, in the conversation with Butler, he based his right to continue to preach in Bristol on the alleged *jus ubique praedicandi* possessed by the Fellow of an Oxford College—and legally he was quite wrong: Fellows had a *jus ubique docendi*, not *praedicandi*; they could teach anywhere, but not preach anywhere. Actually, he based the claim on his divine call. The Bishop was on safe ground, Wesley was on very dangerous ground. But history—if it is allowed to prove anything—proved that Wesley was right.

In London, where Wesley spent most of his time during the very early years of the Revival when he was not in Bristol, things followed much the same course as they had in Bristol. Vast crowds assembled to hear Wesley preach, whether it was in the fields or in the parish churches which still sometimes invited him. The Fetter Lane Society grew rapidly and was organized into Classes. But an important issue came steadily to the fore. In the

Fetter Lane Society there were many Moravians—very naturally, in view of Wesley's close kinship with their leaders. But some of these Moravians began to advance doctrines which Wesley viewed with great repugnance. They made much play with the text 'Be still and know that I am God', and interpreted it and other texts to mean that 'stillness', that is, abstention from Bible reading, corporate prayer, Holy Communion, and even good works, was the duty of every converted man and woman until he was perfectly sanctified. If he indulged in them before that, it was urged, he would think of them as having, 'merit', as earning salvation, whereas salvation comes through the grace of God alone, without any merit on our part. The chief exponent of this somewhat perverse interpretation of the doctrine of Justification by Faith was P. H. Molther, but he seems for a time to have gained the support of leading Moravians, such as Spangenberg and even Zinzendorf, though modern Moravians insist, probably rightly, that Molther's views were at odds with genuine Moravian tenets.

Wesley, then as always, opposed with all his might any disparagement of the 'means of grace', and argued persistently with the Moravians of Fetter Lane. But apparently he did not gain the support of the majority of the Society; he purchased a disused cannon-foundry, turned it into a Society Room and chapel, and started a new, genuinely Methodist Society there. The Foundery Society was at first in fellowship with Fetter Lane, but the increasing 'stillness' of the latter alienated Wesley more and more from it, and fellowship ceased; two years later the Fetter Lane Society became officially a Moravian Society. The Foundery served Wesley as his London headquarters.

Wesley was now ready for the extension of his mission to the rest of the nation, the mission which he constantly described as that of 'spreading scriptural holiness throughout the land'. He was quite clear as to the content of the Gospel which he had been ordained to preach, and he had confirmed it in his own experience; he had tried out his methods of preaching it, and of confirming it in the lives of those to whom he preached, in Bristol and London; the situation with which he had been confronted in those two cities had shown how great was the need which the Gospel was designed to meet. Henceforth no diocesan or episcopal rule was going to prevent him from doing what he conceived to be his plain duty. Not long after his interview with the Bishop of Bristol he wrote to a friend:

> I look upon all the world as my parish; thus far I mean, that, in whatever part of it I am, I judge it meet, right, and my bounden duty to declare unto all that are willing to hear the glad tidings of salvation.

So began the journeyings up and down England, and into Wales, Scotland, and Ireland, which were to cease only at his death. Newcastle upon Tyne was the first city of the north of England to be visited, and the triangle of Bristol, London, and Newcastle formed a convenient groundplan for the development of his strategy. Until he was seventy years old he travelled almost entirely on horse-back, covering four to five thousand miles a year, and sometimes seventy or eighty miles a day. He consistently preached four or five times each day; at every stopping place he set on foot, or inspected and improved, the organization required for caring for the souls of those whom he had influenced. He kept an eye on the financial and spiritual affairs of each Society—many of which contained few people who could read and write—and was in constant correspondence with his helpers up and down the country. But the pattern of evangelism, pastoral care, and discipline which he had worked out in Bristol and London served him in good stead throughout his life, with necessary amplifications, and survived it to form part of the permanent constitution of Methodism all over the world.

But, of course, he did not do all this alone, though the predominant position which he naturally and inevitably attained would have entitled him to say (what he certainly would never have said): '*Le Méthodisme, c'est moi!*' In the early days George Whitefield cooperated closely, though Whitefield's methods were never completely assimilated to Wesley's careful provisions, and he was very frequently out of the country. (He was, in fact, incumbent of the parish church in Savannah, Georgia, but this does not seem to have hampered his activities very much.) Charles Wesley, as we have seen, threw himself heart and soul into evangelistic enterprise; and the far-reaching effect of the hymns which he wrote to support the efforts of all the Methodist preachers will be considered in the next chapter.

Then there was a small group of ordained clergymen who valued Wesley's work and gave it as much support as possible.

William Grimshaw was vicar of Haworth in Yorkshire (and therefore a predecessor of Patrick Brontë) from 1742 until his death in 1763. He ruled his parishioners with a rod of iron, but seems to have had a heart of gold. He preached the Methodist message with fire and fervour in the blunt language which is said to be especially congenial to the people of Yorkshire, and he certainly met with astonishing success in the number of conversions and attendances at Holy Communion recorded. He travelled widely in the West Riding without incurring the excessive wrath of the Archbishop of York (who, however, urged him to be more prudent), was appointed by Wesley to be superintendent of the Haworth Circuit, and died of a fever caught while visiting a sick parishioner.

Vincent Perronet was vicar of Shoreham in Kent, and ten years older than Wesley. He was a man of quiet and studious habit, who stayed in his parish, but was always available to give help and advice to John and Charles, and to defend them in writing against their detractors when needed. He was called the Archbishop or umpire of Methodism, and many disputes were settled in his peaceful parsonage; there also John was occasionally prevailed upon to rest and read for a few days.

A much more fantastic spirit than either of these was John Berridge, vicar of Everton (not in Lancashire, but Bedfordshire) from 1755. He was a good scholar in his Cambridge days, but few traces of this were in evidence when he began his own revival in his parish in 1756. He was not officially linked with the Wesleys, but was in close accord with them, and they thought it best to allow him to conduct his own mission in his own way. The Everton revival, which reached its height in 1759, and spread far over the neighbouring countryside, was accompanied by psychological phenomena even more striking than those at Kingswood. Berridge's language and methods were rough and ready, in comparison with Wesley's precision; in later years he became extravagant in the extreme, and verged on madness. His theology turned gradually towards Calvinism, and away from Wesley's; but on his death-bed he was very willing to agree with a friend who said that Wesley and he would 'unite in perfect harmony in heaven'. 'Ay, ay,' said the old man. 'That we shall, to be sure; for the Lord washed our hearts here, and there He will wash our brains.'

But by the far most gifted, influential, and saintly of all

Wesley's clerical friends—and perhaps of all his friends—was Fletcher of Madeley. Jean Guillaume de la Flechère, born in Switzerland in 1729, the descendant of a noble Savoy family, studied for a while in Geneva, and came to England to learn the language. Now calling himself John William Fletcher, he was appointed tutor to a Shropshire family, and a few months later met Wesley and became a Methodist. Wesley persuaded him in due course to be ordained, and in 1760 he was appointed to the living of Madeley, also in Shropshire. Here he ministered for the rest of his days, a model pastor of his flock, but by his gentleness and charity, his humility and courage, spreading the infection of holiness all through the ranks of the Methodists. Wesley became convinced that if any man on earth could claim to have been granted the gift of 'Perfect Love', it was Fletcher, and urgently wished to designate him as his successor in the acknowledged leadership of the Methodists; but Fletcher, consistently with the whole tenor of his life, refused the honour. He was an acute and lucid theologian, and his *Checks to Antinomianism* takes rank as a classic of courteous theological controversy.

From the nature of the case, these men could not spend their whole time, or even most of their time, itinerating with the Gospel in the manner of Wesley himself. He came to rely more and more, reluctantly at first, but afterwards cheerfully, on preachers who came from every walk of life and often started from very humble origins. It took the insight of his mother to see, and to persuade her son, that Thomas Maxfield, a mere layman, who took it upon himself to preach at the Foundery, was called of God to do so (he may not have been the first lay preacher of Methodism, but his was the test case). But once the principle was established, Wesley, with the inspired opportunism which enabled him to make use of any method—whether he had thought of it himself or not—for furthering his work (we have seen this already in the case of Captain Foy and the 'classes' in the New Room in Bristol), set about training and preparing his lay preachers for the work which he now saw that they would be able to do. He chose them for their personal knowledge of salvation, and at first set a period of one year for their 'probation' (the word is still current in Methodism); later he extended it to four years. During this period they had to follow a course of reading prescribed by him, and were expected to spend five out of every twenty-four hours on this occupation (though they were also, of course, heavily engaged in the business of evangelism and pastoral work). In 1753 the *Twelve Rules of a Helper* (that is, one who had passed successfully through his period of probation) were issued, and include the following:

> ... never be unemployed a moment, never be triflingly employed. Converse sparingly and cautiously with women; particularly with young women in private.... Do not affect the gentleman. You have no more to do with this character than with that of a dancing-master. A Preacher of the Gospel is the servant of all. Be ashamed of nothing but sin: not of fetching wood (if time permit), or drawing water; not of cleaning your own shoes, or your neighbours'. Be punctual. Do everything exactly at the time. And, in general, do not mend our rules, but keep them. You have nothing to do but to save souls. Therefore, spend and be spent in the work. Observe. It is not your business to preach so many times ... but to save as many souls as you can. Therefore, you will need all the sense you have, and to have your wits about you.

Men who obeyed these rules were clearly a force to be reckoned with.

John Nelson (1707–74) was a stonemason from Yorkshire, converted by Wesley in London. At first he travelled with Wesley, but afterwards was entrusted by him with the beginnings of Methodist work in Leeds, Manchester, Sheffield, and York (still small towns then, of course). He endured incredible hardships, and much violence from anti-Methodist mobs; his enemies arranged for him to be press-ganged into the army, and he finally escaped this only after years of petty persecution. John Haime (1710–84), on the other hand, welcomed the chance of preaching the Gospel in the army and founding Methodist Societies there; he was opposed by the chaplains, but supported by the Commander-in-Chief, the Duke of Cumberland. Thomas Olivers (1725–99) came from Montgomeryshire; he lost his position as a shoemaker's apprentice by bad behaviour, but was converted by George Whitefield, and educated himself. His hymn 'The God of Abraham praise' shows a deep understanding of Scripture; he obtained a tune for it from Leoni, who was a chorister in the Great Synagogue in Duke's Place, London.

Howell Harris (1714–73) was a helper of Wesley's in a different sense. He came from Trevecca in Breconshire, and was a Welshman through and through. He was intended for Anglican Orders, but after a profound religious experience in 1735 he became a free-lance evangelist to his own countrymen. He was suspicious of Wesley's good faith when he first heard of his Bristol activities, but after coming to hear him became his warm advocate. But his sympathies were with Whitefield's theology rather than Wesley's, and when the two leaders disagreed he cast in his lot with Whitefield. Yet he and Wesley were never personally estranged, and Wesley was content to leave to him and his helpers the task of evangelizing Wales, and rarely visited that country himself. Harris founded a college for future preachers at Trevecca, with the strong backing of Whitefield and his patroness, the Countess of Huntingdon, and Fletcher was President of it until the controversy about predestination drove him from its doors.

Wesley had many women helpers; in fact, women participated freely in all the activities of the eighteenth-century Methodists in a manner which would have shocked their nineteenth-century contemporaries. Foremost among them was undoubtedly Mary Bosanquet (1739–1815). She was brought up in comfortable circumstances, but the influence of the Methodists caused her to devote her life to the care of the underprivileged. For a number of years she ran an orphanage in her own home, and later became a preacher. In fact, in 1787 she was authorized as an itinerant preacher in the Methodist Connexion 'so long as she preaches our doctrine and attends to our discipline'. In 1781 John Fletcher proposed marriage to her; he had decided some twenty-five years previously that if he ever married she would be the right wife; but since at that time, and for many years afterwards, she had money of her own, he forbore to propose, lest his real motive for doing so be his desire for her money. But by now she was impoverished by her works of charity, and he could be satisfied that his motives were pure. She accepted the proposal, and watched over him patiently and tenderly during the last years of his life, which were grievously stricken by illness and feebleness.

It would serve no useful purpose to detail the fierce opposition which Wesley and his lieutenants encountered as soon as their work got into full swing and became widely known. Some of it sprang from reasonable doubts as to the wisdom of his unconventional methods and the effectiveness of his apparently untrained assistants, as well as from questions about the orthodoxy of his theology. Much of it came from sheer jealousy and malice. Among the sober and reasonable attacks must be counted that of Josiah Tucker, the humane and progressive Dean of Gloucester, who blamed the errors and extravagances of Wesley on the teaching of William Law—in a sense, with good reason. Personal attacks on Wesley labelled him as hypocrite, libertine, Papist, Jacobite—and most insistently of all, '*enthusiast*'. Lavington, Bishop of Exeter, gave ample excuse to the tribe of lewd pamphleteers by the distempered nastiness of his *The Enthusiasm of the Methodists and Papists compared.* But since he himself was forced to admit some years later the inaccuracy of his charges, we need not dwell on them. Wesley's custom was to pass over the great majority of such diatribes in silence, and only to answer those which might do harm to the Methodists at large by reason of their authoritative origin. Lavington therefore received a stern and crushing, but not discourteous, reply.

Mob violence was encountered chiefly during the early years of the Revival; after 1751 it died away altogether. It was mostly stimulated by clergy and squires who thought that Wesley was giving the lower classes ideas above their station, and sometimes arose from the real but entirely unfounded conviction that Wesley was stirring up rebellion against proper authority. The hiring of a gang to break up a Methodist meeting was quite a commonplace for some years, and sometimes the ensuing proceedings developed into a mortal threat. Not only John Wesley, but his brother Charles and several others from among the preachers, were more than once within an inch of their life. It was Wesley's practice 'to look a mob in the face'. This was sometimes so immediately effective that the mob just melted away. At other times this did not happen so easily, but on no occasion did Wesley show any sign of the panic that would have given the mob its chance; and every time he came out victorious in the end. One example of his courage will indicate how the matter usually went. This is the entry in the *Journal* for 4 July 1745:

I rode to Falmouth. About three in the afternoon I went to see a gentlewoman who had long been indisposed. Almost as soon as I was sat down, the house was beset on all sides by an unnumerable multitude of people. A louder or more confused noise could hardly be at the taking of a city by storm. At first Mrs B. and her daughter endeavoured to quiet them. But it was labour lost. They might as well have attempted to still the raging of the sea.... The rabble roared with all their throats; 'Bring out the Canorum! Where is the Canorum?' (An unmeaning word which the Cornish generally use instead of Methodist.)

No answer being given, they quickly forced open the outer door, and filled the passage. Only a wainscot partition was between us, which was not likely to stand long. I immediately took down a large looking-glass which hung against it, supposing the whole side would fall in at once. When they began their work, with abundance of bitter imprecations, poor Kitty (the maid) was utterly astonished, and cried out: 'O, sir, what must we do?' I said: 'We must pray.' Indeed at that time, to all appearance, our lives were not worth an hour's purchase.... Among those without were the crews of some privateers, which were lately come into harbour. Some of these, being angry at the slowness of the rest, thrust them away, and coming up all together, set their shoulders to the inner door, and cried out: 'Avast, lads, avast!' Away went all the hinges at once, and the door fell back into the room.

I stepped forward at once into the midst of them, and said: 'Here I am. Which of you has anything to say to me? To which of you have I done any wrong? To you? Or to you? Or you?' I continued speaking till I came, bare-headed as I was (for I purposely left my hat that they might all see my face), into the middle of the street, and then raising my voice, said: 'Neighbours, countrymen! Do you desire to hear me speak?' They cried vehemently: 'Yes, yes! He shall speak! He shall! Nobody shall hinder him!' But having nothing to stand on, and no advantage of ground, I could be heard by few only. However, I spoke without intermission, and, as far as the sound reached, the people were still; till one or two of their captains turned about and swore, not a man should touch him.

The development of the Revival was not hampered by either verbal or physical violence. Wesley went serenely on with his work while the rabble raged. Much more serious was the internal strife which from time to time broke out among his supporters. As often happens at a time of spiritual awakening, some people joined the movement because of the sensations that they might expect to receive. If they are disappointed in this, such people go off to start religious movements on their own. This happened once or twice in the growth of Methodism, and there were some also who quarrelled with Wesley because of thwarted personal ambition. But by and large, his strong personality prevented outbursts of personal feeling. What he could not prevent was theological controversy.

Whitefield was convinced that God had from eternity pre-destined the majority of mankind to damnation, and a few to salvation through Jesus Christ. The purpose of his evangelistic activity was to gather to Christ those who were pre-destined to salvation. It is true that while he was preaching there was no hint that only some of his audience had any chance of responding to his appeal; in fact, it seems highly likely that for the time being he forgot his own doctrine in his passionate gratitude for the love of God to sinners. But the doctrine was there all the same, and he was prepared to defend it to the end. Many of the early Methodists agreed with him—which was not at all surprising, for they were nurtured, many of them, in the Puritan tradition, and most of the Puritans had believed as strongly as Calvin in the 'decree to be shuddered at'* (Calvin's own name for it). Moreover, the great Selina, Countess of Huntingdon, believed in it too, and gave her personal backing to all who preached it.

The Countess did not rule her circle of friends and supporters by reason of any physical beauty or charm, but by a combination of high birth, wealth, natural authority, graciousness, single-mindedness, and pertinacity. She was first influenced in the direction of seriousness by Benjamin Ingham, one time member of the Holy Club, and she was in the London Methodist Societies from the beginning. She persuaded a fair number of her aristocratic friends that Methodists were not necessarily mad, or at least induced them to come to her *salons* to hear the more acceptable of them. Her husband, the ninth Earl, was inclined to restrain her religious exuberance, lest it burst the bounds of refined behaviour, but he died too soon to do so effectively. Selina, after his death in 1746, selected the Methodist preachers whom she thought the polite world ought to hear, and frequently built chapels for them to preach in. She was, of course, the chief benefactress of Trevecca College.

Both the Wesleys rejected predestination root and branch. They were quite sure that Christ had really and truly died for all men. 'For all, for all, my Saviour died' was the burden of one

* *'Decretum quidem horrendum.'*

of Charles's most frequently sung hymns. The restriction of God's grace to the elect few was utterly repugnant to their understanding of the New Testament, and made nonsense of the moral and spiritual life. They agreed that the initiative in salvation was wholly God's, and that faith itself was the gift of God; but they refused to draw from this the conclusion that man was denied the free choice between damnation and salvation.

The argument between the two parties broke out soon after the beginning of the Revival, but it was kept within bounds by the agreement between Whitefield and John Wesley that the two principals should not engage in public controversy, and that each should work in his own sphere without interruption from the other. But the expulsion of six Methodists of the Calvinistic persuasion from St Edmund Hall, Oxford, in 1768 set the controversy alight, and many of the Calvinistic pamphlets were directed personally against John Wesley. In the van of the attack was Augustus Montague Toplady, and his words about Wesley were so vitriolic that his opponent momentarily lost his habitual calm and answered back by publishing a highly tendentious summary of Toplady's argument, over the intials A— T—. This precipitated a further flood of abuse from Toplady and his associate, Rowland Hill; the Minutes of Wesley's Conference in 1770 took an uncompromising line; and Whitefield's death in the same year removed the last restraints. All anti-Calvinists were removed from Trevecca, and the controversy pursued an unedifying path, though Wesley gave no further encouragement to it. Toplady, perhaps fortunately, is better known to later generations for his authorship of the hymn 'Rock of Ages' (traditionally, but probably not really, written in a storm in Burrington Combe, near Cheddar, while the author was sheltering under the rock of that name), than for his controversial spleen. When he published the hymn he pointed out that, according to a reasonable calculation, everyone who lived to be eighty committed 2,522,880,000 sins. It is to be hoped that he was thinking of his own sins, as well as of those of Mr Wesley, who was approaching eighty at the time.

The nett result of all this was that Lady Huntingdon's preachers became quite separate from Wesley's, and were loosely organized into 'Lady Huntingdon's Connexion', which became in the course of the years, with the decay of predestinarian doctrine, a number of almost disconnected Congregational Churches. Howel Harris's followers in Wales were organized into the Calvinistic Methodist Church, which has changed its name during the present century to the Presbyterian Church of Wales.

A by-product of the argument about predestination was the one about Antinomianism. Some of the Methodists with Calvinistic views, but by no means all, contended that when a man is justified by faith, 'complete righteousness' is imputed to him, and can never be cancelled or impaired whatever he does or however many sins he commits; they believed, that is, in a 'finished salvation' which involved no good works of any sort at any point. Wesley, of course, held that good works and holiness are the necessary result of justification, and that a man, once justified, must 'work for the meat that endureth to everlasting life'. Wesley's views on this point were expounded in the Minutes of his Conference in 1770, and aroused fierce opposition from the Antinomians. Fletcher took up the cudgels on Wesley's behalf, and his *Checks to Antinomianism* furnish the official Wesleyan answer to it. He points out the immorality and hypocrisy that are bound to result from the antinomian view, and urges that even before justification repentance is a necessary 'condition' of salvation, though of course it does not *merit* salvation; and that after justification every believer must go on to sanctification, and will be rewarded at the last day on the evidence of the good works he has done since he was justified. This controversy did not have so disruptive an effect as the main one with the predestinarians, but it consumed much time and energy.

Through all the years of persecution and strife Wesley was perfecting the organization of his Societies. They were grouped early on into 'Circuits', very large at first, and gradually decreasing in size as the movement advanced. After 1784 the representatives of each Society in the Circuit met once a quarter, and soon came to issue each quarter a 'Plan' of the preachers appointed from week to week in each Society. Wesley retained the general control of all the Circuits as their 'Superintendent', but appointed an 'Assistant' to each of them; these 'Assistants' came to be called Superintendents. It gradually became customary for a preacher to stay in a Circuit for three years, though Wesley at first thought that even this was too long. It has been suggested that the 'three-year system' was copied from that which obtained in Customs and Excise (for obvious reasons), and it would be wholly in accord with Wesley's genius to copy such secular institutions as seemed to meet his purpose. But it is more likely that he calculated that a preacher would have preached to the same congregation all that he usefully could in about three years. In 1744 he began the practice of calling together his clerical supporters and his preachers to a Conference. Inevitably this gathering became annual, and settled the main affairs of the 'Connexion' (as it came to be called) for the ensuing year.

At the same time the Societies developed their devotional and liturgical practices. The 'preaching service', held at a different time from the services of the Parish Church, became exceedingly popular. Love-feasts, the revival of the New Testament '*Agape*', were borrowed from the Moravians and widely practised, at first by members of the 'bands' only, and later by all members of the Society. Each person present received a piece of plain cake and a cup of water, and these were taken together in token of fellowship. Afterwards, each one present, if possible, gave a testimony to God's power and love, and many hymns were sung. Most characteristically Methodist of all was the 'Covenant Service'. It originated in one of the London Societies when Wesley read the words of the Covenant which Richard Alleine, the Puritan, had suggested that every Christian should make with his Lord. Methodists all over the country began to repeat it, and it became an annual institution for the first Sunday of the year. The practice stills hold, and every Methodist is expected to assent to the demanding words :

> Christ has many services to be done : some are easy, others are difficult; some bring honour, others bring reproach; some are suitable to our natural inclinations and temporal interests, others are contrary to both. In some we may please Christ and please ourselves, in others we cannot please Christ except by denying ourselves. Yet the power to do all these things is assuredly given us in Christ, who strengtheneth us. Therefore let us make the Covenant of God our own. Let us engage our heart to the Lord, and resolve in His strength never to go back. . . .

and to take upon his lips this prayer :

> I am no longer my own, but Thine. Put me to what Thou wilt, rank me with whom Thou wilt; put me to doing, put me to suffer-

ing; let me be employed for Thee or laid aside for Thee, exalted for Thee or brought low for Thee; let me be full, let me be empty; let me have all things, let me have nothing; I freely and heartily yield all things to Thy pleasure and disposal. And now, O glorious and blessed God, Father, Son and Holy Spirit, Thou art mine, and I am Thine. So be it. And the Covenant which I have made on earth, let it be ratified in heaven.

Nothing more clearly expresses the *personal* nature of Methodist piety.

Wesley was well aware that his people were for the most part uneducated—not through lack of ability, but through lack of opportunity; and he had a strong sense of the value of education to religion. He became, in fact, one of the pioneers of popular education in England. He wrote numerous books and pamphlets for paperback sale; he issued cheap editions of many classics. He founded schools in many places, and encouraged others to do the same. The most important and permanent of his educational enterprises was Kingswood School. He inherited from Whitefield in the early days a school for the sons of colliers in Kingswood Chase. This was not a great success, and was replaced by a much more ambitious design. A school was opened on the same site for the sons of Methodists who wished their boys to be rescued from the laxity, barbarity, and idleness prevalent in the boarding-schools of the day (however eminent they may have become in later history), and were willing to have them taken off their hands completely, and thoroughly trained in body, mind, and soul, without holidays or relaxation. The programme was a formidable one, and suffered many setbacks; Wesley thought of boys as sinful adults in all but age. But he learned from experience, and succeeded in creating by trial and error (and many expulsions of boys and masters) something which he could proudly call a 'Christian family', founded on the educational principles which he had received from his mother. The school was opened in 1748 'to the glory of God, the best and greatest, and the service of Church and State'.* Charles Wesley's hymn, written for the occasion, was sung, containing the lines:

* John Jones, the first real 'Headmaster' of the School, was third in the Methodist hierarchy to John and Charles Wesley during the 1750s and 1760s.

Unite the pair, so long disjoined,
Knowledge and vital piety...

Kingswood School was later limited to the sons of Methodist preachers, but this restriction has long been abandoned.

John Wesley did not confine his interest and his activities to the welfare of the Methodists. He took 'the whole world as his parish' in more than one sense. He was greatly concerned by the terrible conditions, for instance, in which French prisoners-of-war were kept in Bristol, and took steps to help them; he campaigned for the improvement of prisons in general; he opened dispensaries for the sick poor, and published his own treatise on *Primitive Physick* (an up-to-date document by the standard of the times); he took steps to counteract the activities of smugglers in Cornwall, where his influence was especially great; and, above all, his last years were marked by his determined support of those who were trying to abolish 'that execrable villainy, the scandal of religion, of England, and of human nature, slavery'.* In fact, in only one great issue did he fail to take the side which subsequent generations have recognized to be the progressive one: he supported the English government in its attempt to quell the rebellion of the American colonies.

When he died at the age of eighty-eight, having preached and travelled almost to the last, he could look back on the achievement of his plans in nearly every field, in spite of all opposition, in a manner granted to few men, even the greatest. He had affected for good the whole life of England to an extent which all must recognize though none can calculate. And he had built up the strength of his own Methodist family to 72,000 members (though the Societies were purged each year of those who did not entirely make the grade) in England, and to nearly as many beyond the seas. He could justly claim that all of these were converted to God, and living lives of service to God and their fellow men in the pursuit of holiness.

And what sort of people had he helped them to become? There were 'not many wise after the flesh, not many mighty, not many noble', as St Paul says of the Church in Corinth. The Methodists were mostly from what was once called the

* His *Thoughts Upon Slavery* (1774) was perhaps the first reasoned attack on slavery by a man of influence.

working class; but many came from the ranks of shopkeepers, and the effect of practising the Methodist virtues was to send all of them steadily up the social scale, so that Wesley warns them frequently in his later sermons of the dangers of wealth. They were frugal, industrious, conscientious, sabbatarian; strict, and sometimes narrow and prudish, in their morals; stern in the bringing up of their children; averse from entertainments and unrestrained laughter. So far they were staunch representatives of the Puritan tradition which has never died out in England, unless it has done so recently. But those who had really caught the meaning of Wesley's message had something else about them also: an inward, serene gaiety which comes out over and over again in Charles Wesley's hymns, springing from the joyful assurance of salvation which Calvinism fails to give. And, as a result, the Methodists knew not only how to face hardship and scorn without being much troubled, but also how to die.

CHAPTER FIVE

The Theology and the Hymns of the Revival

The popular image of an evangelist, and still more of a revivalist, is a man with a crude, ill-thought-out, hell-fire theology, who alternately wheedles and terrifies his hearers into accepting his message; the theology he is thought to have taken over ready-made from some literalist interpreter of the Bible; his emotionalism is believed to spring from a defect in his own personality. There have indeed been revivalists and evangelists of whom these criticisms have been perfectly just, and some of them have added to their ill-fame an undue financial astuteness. These men have brought discredit on the honourable enterprise of evangelism, without which there could have been no Christian Church and can be no expansion of its influence. But, so far at least as Great Britain is concerned, they all came after the time of the Wesleys, and it would be unhistorical in the extreme to have the modern evangelist-image in one's mind when studying the Methodist Revival.

John Wesley was a theologian before he became an evangelist, and he remained a theologian all through the years of his evangelistic mission. In fact, it would be true to say that his primary interest never ceased to be theological, since it was by the exposition of Scriptural truth that he brought men and women to the point of repentance and faith, and after they had been converted he continued to see that they were instructed in Scriptural truth to the end of their days. Christian doctrine was for him no mere means to the end of emotional conversion; it was the truth which made men free, and he devoted his best powers of mind and spirit all through his life to its understanding and proclamation. Emotionalism he despised as much as any modern sceptic, though of course the modern sceptic would always see emotionalism where Wesley saw the operation of the Holy Spirit. A casual glance at any one of his published sermons—and these were the sermons, perhaps embellished by some illustrations, by which people were converted in their hundreds—will show how little Wesley valued an emotional appeal, and how much he valued theological exposition.

He did not expound the whole corpus of Christian doctrine; there is hardly a sermon or treatise from his pen on the Trinity, or on Christology, or on the deity of the Holy Spirit. The reason for this silence is simple: he took for granted the truth of the doctrines of the Creed, and busied himself with those among them, and those resulting from them, which were immediately relevant to man's salvation. Elaborate, well-documented attempts have been made in great numbers to prove that Wesley's doctrines of the Person of Christ, of God the Creator, of the Trinity, and many other matters, were completely catholic. They have all succeeded in doing so without any difficulty, and they are elaborate only because the evidence for their contention has to be gleaned from allusions and casual references. Wesley, as a practical man, did not spend time in expounding what had been perfectly well expounded by others.

But the case was different when it came to showing how God deals with the sinners for whom Christ died. This side of doctrine had been, in his judgement, shamefully neglected, and in any case had to be stated again and again to those who needed to know it and for those whose task it was to preach it. As he himself put it, he was concerned to find out and proclaim 'the way to heaven', and it is with 'the way to heaven' that his published sermons are almost entirely occupied.

He based his theology on the Bible and 'experience', but far more on the Bible than on experience. The Bible was for him the 'book of God', and he placed implicit trust in all its statements. When any passage was obscure to him, he compared it with other more lucid passages, and so arrived at what he took to be its true meaning. He quotes Scripture in much the same way as a modern fundamentalist does, but this does not mean that he was a fundamentalist in the modern sense. He lived before the days of modern Biblical criticism, and so can hardly be expected to have taken its findings into account. He was not aware of the sources which lie behind the Pentateuch, or of the theory that there is more than one author of the prophecy of Isaiah, or of the Synoptic problem; he did not question the traditional view that the purpose of prophecy is to delineate the future and he eagerly accepted a theory of the meaning of the Book of Revelation which turned it into a kind of Old Moore's Almanack of the last year of human existence. But in all these matters he was in complete accord with the other theologians of his time. It was not that, like the modern fundamentalist, he had heard of the critical theories of the Bible and rejected them; he had never heard of them because they had not been put forward. If it is asked whether he would have accepted them if he had heard of them, no answer is possible. It might be thought that he would perhaps have been cautious in his approach to them; but it is very unlikely that with his lively, inquisitive mind, which kept abreast with the latest scientific discoveries, with a special eye to the use that could be made of them for human welfare, he would have rejected them out of hand. At any rate, when he came to write his *Notes on the New Testament* he made extensive use of—in fact, he largely borrowed—the work of the most acute of pre-critical scholars, Johannes Albrecht Bengel, whose *Gnomon Novi Testamenti*, a concise exegesis of the whole New Testament, appeared in 1734.

On the basis of his study of the Bible he produced a coherent body of doctrine on the subject nearest to his heart, the salvation of mankind, and the significant fact is that the Scriptural exegesis in which it is grounded is ruled out by modern scholarship at very few points. For the most part it is a Biblical theology which may, indeed, be erroneous, but is as tenable today by serious theologians as it was in his own time. His literalism did not prevent him from penetrating to the core of the Biblical message, whereas modern literalism tends to do exactly that.

The Methodist emphasis on 'religious experience' is well-known in religious circles, and is of course very vulnerable to psychological attack. But it is only in small part derived from Wesley. He never based a single doctrine on it, but always appealed to Scripture. If, however, a doctrine was propounded by Scripture and therefore trustworthy, he was willing to show that it was confirmed by experience—which is, of course, a respectably traditional method of establishing a proposition. Still less did he found any doctrine on 'feelings'. Charles Wesley says a great deal about feelings in his hymns, in such phrases as 'My God, I know, I feel Thee mine', and seems to lay great emphasis on them. But he did not mean by this word mere emotions; he refers, rather, to that consciousness of personal relationship or of truth which comes to the whole personality, and not to the mind and senses alone, nor even chiefly to the mind and senses —he means what in the case of the poet is sometimes called 'imaginative awareness'. John certainly never sought to prove a religious truth by feelings in the modern restricted sense; feelings in the fuller sense were part of what he meant by experience, and of what caused him constantly to refer to real Christianity as 'experimental (we should say *experiential*) religion'. 'Experience,' wrote John Wesley, 'is properly alleged to confirm' doctrine.

The Methodist misunderstanding of Methodism in this matter is due, perhaps, to historical causes. It came to be widely sensed by Methodist teachers during the second half of the nineteenth century that the Bible was under fire—people sensed this long before they seriously studied the attacks of the critics. But the Bible was the source of all their doctrine; what were they to do if the Bible was taken from them? (It has to be remembered that Christians argued at that time that if one statement in the Bible were shown to be false, the whole Bible was undermined.) The best thing to do was to fall back on experience, which Biblical critics could not touch; and so experience gradually took over the place of the Bible as the source of doctrine. Little did its champions know that experience is much more open to attack, from theology as well as from psychology, than the Bible. But this was before the days of Karl Barth as well as of Freud.

Wesley's question, then, was: what does the Scripture teach about the way to heaven? The answer can be fully and clearly set out. Adam was created in God's image, holy, merciful, perfect; he was taught the perfect moral law of love, and given the power to choose between good and evil. He used his freedom to disobey God, lost the image of God, and received the image of the Devil. From this time forward the thoughts and desires of Adam, and through him of the whole human race, were wholly impure, self-willed, and idolatrous. This is Original Sin, and every man and woman since the time of Adam has been born with the guilt of it already on him. So man is condemned to pain and suffering—before the Fall these things did not exist—and to death, death of the body, and hereafter death of the soul in hell.

This relentless teaching about man and sin is, however, alleviated by the consideration that fallen man still has the law of God written on his heart, and a conscience with which to discern it. He knows what is right, but he is unable to do it. The first effect of such knowledge is to indicate to him the terrible doom which his sin incurs; but, since the purposes of God even in condemnation are loving, it goes on to show him his urgent need of Jesus Christ, and leads him towards Him. The Methodist preachers were always instructed by Wesley to preach the Law first, and then the Gospel, the Law to open men's eyes to their dreadful predicament and then to show them the way of escape, the Gospel to enable them to use it. Conscience is the gift of God —sometimes Wesley calls it 'prevenient grace'—and it shows that God is at work even in depraved man for his salvation. So also is reason, and reason is not entirely withdrawn from fallen man. And he has another gift of God, perhaps the most precious gift of all, freedom. This freedom is not the natural right of fallen man. On the contrary, man forfeited his right to freedom, along with all his other rights, when he fell into sin. But God, of His mercy, has given us a measure of freedom, and by His grace we are able to perform our duty, and above all to hear and receive the Word of God. A man who refuses God's forgiveness when it is offered to him through Christ refuses of his own free will; there is no question of predestination to be a 'vessel of wrath'.

But all this so far is a mere preamble to Wesley's real message. He had no delight in speaking of the Fall and doom of man, or of the small remnant of God's gifts still left with him. He referred to these matters only because otherwise the announcement of God's grace would be made *in vacuo*; he had to remind his hearers of the situation which elicited the divine mercy. But it is with the divine mercy and grace that he is really concerned. Nothing that man has ever done, or can possibly do, bestows any merit of any kind on man—Wesley will not agree that all good works done before a man is justified are 'splendid sins', as the Calvinists were inclined to call them; they come in some way from the divine grace, and have some virtue, though they are not done as God wills good works to be done. But they confer no merit at all, and it is the very depth and height of blasphemy to suggest that man in any sense *deserves* the grace of God. Grace is wholly unmerited. It is a scarcely lesser blasphemy to say that the grace of God is limited to certain select or elect persons. It is free for all and to all. The grace of God is the centrepiece of the whole Wesleyan theology.

How is God's grace bestowed upon us? It still comes as something of a surprise, even an unwelcome surprise, to the present-day followers of Wesley to be told that he believed in baptismal regeneration. But he certainly did, so far as infant baptism was concerned. He recognized that this belief was part of Anglican doctrine, accepted it as being based on Scripture, and was prepared to defend it against its critics. The baptism of infants was the washing away of original sin by the Holy Ghost. It is, in fact, the first and in some ways the clearest manifestation of the grace of God which comes to a human being; for it is very certain that the infant when he is baptized has done nothing to deserve the washing away of his sin.

But it must be admitted that infant baptism was of very little effective use to anyone except those (numerous enough until the twentieth century) who died before reaching the age of actual sin. For the effect of actual sin, which everyone commits, is steadily to obliterate the benefits of baptism. This normally happens fairly early in life, though Wesley once, in a fit of unusual optimism about himself, said that he did not think that it had completely happened to him before the age of ten; and it happens to everyone who stays alive long enough. When it has happened, a man is in the same parlous state through actual sin as he was previously through original sin. At this point in his life, as at all times, 'grace is the source, faith the condition, of salvation'. The supreme gift of grace is Jesus Christ. He lived a perfect life, suffered, and died, and so achieved supreme merit in the eyes of God, though of course He did not need to do so. His supreme merit is put down to our account, and we are saved by the merits of Christ. Of course, Wesley ought not to have allowed that even the merits of Christ had any effect on God, if he was to be completely consistent and completely true to his own doctrine of the grace of God; for he is now acknowledging that salvation is in a sense the reward of merit. But this would perhaps have struck him as a piece of hairsplitting, and it certainly does not invalidate his contention that in relation to man God's acts of love are wholly undeserved.

It is by faith that we accept salvation. In an expansive mood Wesley indicates various kinds of faith, which, being purely intellectual, do not avail one whit towards salvation. But he does this only in order to distinguish with the greater sharpness the faith that saves. This faith advances through two stages, he says. There is the 'faith of a servant', his own faith before 24 May 1738, presumably. A man with faith of this order shows it by 'working righteousness', and in virtue of it he is accepted by God. But God wishes him to have a better faith than this, or rather to proceed from this to a better faith, the 'faith of a son'. This faith is a 'disposition of the heart', not just a 'train of ideas'. It is 'a sure trust and confidence that Christ died for *my* sins, that he loved *me* and gave Himself for *me*'. Such faith necessarily includes repentance for past sins, and it is a gift of God, which God wants all men to have.

It is not too much to say that this deeply personal conception of faith was one of the great mainsprings of the Revival. It is easy enough to pervert it into individualism, or to accuse it of being individualistic. But Wesley himself did everything possible, as we shall see, to guard against such a perversion and such a misunderstanding. It is right to point out the objectivity of truth, the otherness of God, the corporateness of New Testament Christianity, and its high doctrine of the Church—and Wesley was to the fore in doing so. But when the prophets of objectivity and corporateness have said all that they truly have to say, the fact remains that if the necessity of personal trust in God is denied, the New Testament loses its meaning and relevance; and Methodism certainly ceases to exist.

In response to saving faith, God justifies us. There is nowhere in Wesley the meticulous argumentation as to whether justification is the 'imputing' or the 'infusing' of righteousness, which has gone on ceaselessly between Protestants and Roman Catholics since the days of Luther. Wesley says that justification simply means pardon; when we are justified, we are 'loved and blessed by God, as if we had never sinned'. And when we are pardoned, the image of God is restored to us, we are adopted as God's sons; in two words, we are 'born again'. The new birth is an elemental event—'a vast inward change, a change wrought in the soul, by the operation of the Holy Ghost'; it means our translation into a quite new world, so that whereas, like an unborn baby, we previously had eyes and ears, but could neither hear nor see, now, like a baby born into the world, we see and hear the things of God. We are alive, whereas before we were dead.

Once we are saved in this way, we can know that we are

saved. And here we enter the highly debatable territory of Wesley's doctrine of 'assurance'. On the authority of Romans 8, 16, he asserts that the Holy Spirit witnesses to (a better translation would have given him 'with') our spirit that we are the children of God; and naturally the witness of the Holy Spirit is incontestable. Therefore we are 'assured' that we have received the pardon of God and are born again. For a long time Wesley and his preachers asserted that unless a man had this assurance he was simply not pardoned by God at all; but he came to see the extravagance of this notion, and confessed that he wondered that he and his brother had not been stoned for uttering it. But he thought to the end that assurance was one of God's normal gifts to His children.

No great imagination is required to see the abuses to which such a doctrine could and did lead. It struck (as it still strikes) respectable Christians as revolting that any man who might have been a drunkard or a thief until the previous week should be encouraged to claim that the Holy Spirit had told him that he was saved. Such feelings spring perhaps from spiritual snobbery, but it was certainly quite possible that such a man might be mistaking his own ebullient feelings, induced by liberation from guilt, for the voice of the Spirit; there was an even greater possibility that the permission to make such claims would lead to spiritual pride of a very unpleasant kind. In practice, Wesley gave short shrift to the claims of humbugs; and he told his followers that the mark, and the only test, of genuine assurance was a changed life. The difficulty remains; yet who would deny that God sometimes gives to men and women who love Him a serene assurance that He is their Father, which no disaster or temptation can ever shake? This is what Wesley was seeking to express, though he used such formalistic terms.

We have seen that Wesley was impressed by the necessity for Christian holiness before the problem of justification and forgiveness presented itself to him. He had to learn that holiness is impossible until forgiveness and justification had been granted, and that so far he had been putting the cart before the horse. But this does not mean that once he was convinced of the need for justification he abandoned the quest for holiness. Quite the contrary was the case. He became, if anything, more zealous for holiness than he had been before—perhaps because he was more successful in the quest; and, what is more important for our present purpose, he insisted that everyone whose sins were forgiven should immediately proceed to sanctification. He was perfectly sincere in his intention 'to spread scriptural holiness throughout the land'; anyone who stopped short at justification put his justification in serious doubt. No falser picture of Wesley has ever been painted than that of the lightning evangelist who appeals to people's emotions, induces them in this way to believe that everything is right between them and God—and then moves on to the next town. Those who insist that men are justified by grace through faith, and not by any good works that they have put to their account, are often criticized for denying the value of spiritual discipline and the moral life. This criticism may be true in some cases—but it is very far from being true of Wesley. Some of his degenerate followers have interpreted his emphasis on the grace of God to imply that once they have received that grace there is simply nothing to be done except wait for automatic admission to heaven; but if they had practised this notion in Wesley's day, they would soon have found themselves outside the Methodist Societies. They would have labelled themselves as 'Antinomians', for whom, as we know, Wesley had little respect.

Unfortunately he sets out on the wrong foot when he begins to expound his doctrine of holiness. He says—and nothing ever induced him to stop saying—that a man whose sins are forgiven does not sin. He was sure that Scripture, in the shape of I John 3, 9,* compelled him to make this statement; he even claimed that experience bore it out. Of course, when he was speaking on this subject, he used a narrow definition of sin, as 'an actual, voluntary transgression of the law'—he was not concerned with inward sins, or evil desires, or hidden defects of character. He freely concedes that believers make mistakes of fact, that in time of illness they give way to sudden temptation, that they sometimes feel frustrated, even that they are sometimes surprised into a sudden action which on further reflection they would not have done. But when they are in full possession of their health and think what they are doing, they do not commit any outward violation of the law of God.

The impression of incredible *naïveté* which this doctrine makes is, however, gradually obliterated as we read Wesley's description of the Christian's growth in grace. Here he is working with a

* 'He that is born of God does not commit sin.'

much wider definition of sin; he thinks of it now as 'the seeds of pride and vanity, of anger, lust, and evil desire', as 'a heart bent to backsliding, a natural tendency to evil, a proneness to depart from God and cleave to the things of earth'. By the work of the Holy Spirit, received, like all God's gifts, by faith, sin in this sense is gradually purged away until a man loves God with all his heart and mind and soul and strength, and his neighbour as himself, until 'God is the joy of his heart and the desire of his soul'. When this point is reached, he is 'perfect in love'; and perfection of love is purity of intention, dedicating all the life to God.

> It is the giving God all our hearts; it is one desire and design ruling all our tempers. It is the devoting, not a part, but all, our soul, body and substance to God. In another view, it is all the mind which was in Christ, enabling us to walk as Christ walked. It is the circumcision of the heart from all filthiness, all inward as well as outward pollution. It is a renewal of the heart in the whole image of God, the full likeness of him that created it.

There is no doubt that Wesley believed it to be possible to reach this 'Christian Perfection', this 'Entire Sanctification', this 'Perfect Love', in this life; what is more, he taught his followers to expect to reach it, though he never claimed to have reached it himself and was usually (not always) rather sceptical of those who did make the claim. He seems to have thought that the usual way of reaching it was by a long and gradual growth, marked by the punctilious performance of God's law, not only in its outward aspects, but still more in its deepest implications as Jesus revealed them in the Sermon on the Mount; and then by a sudden receiving of the 'great salvation' which God has in store for those who love Him. Curiously enough, though he spoke of 'perfection' very freely, he always limited its meaning by teaching that it can be lost after it has been gained, and that those who have it continue to grow in grace to all eternity.

All types of perfectionism are abhorrent to many Christians, including the Lutherans and those nourished in the sobriety of Anglicanism. But Wesley's version of it is to be very sharply distinguished from that of those who say that perfection comes in a moment, soon after conversion, and that it can never be lost; such teaching leads straight to self-righteousness and unteachableness, and it cannot be said that Methodists on the whole have been more liable to those sins than other Christians. It is to be distinguished also from the teaching of those who make perfection an ideal to be sought and gained in solitude, or in the congenial atmosphere of a cloistered community. Wesley's 'perfection', if it came at all, came to those who were busily occupied in worldly affairs. And it was, above all, a *social* perfection. It included the practice of fellowship within the Christian community and the steady, active love of one's neighbour, including one's enemies; it worked itself out in unceasing endeavour to feed the hungry, relieve the sick, care for the prisoner—to carry out, in fact, Wesley's injunction: 'Do all the good you can in all the ways you can, as long as you can.'

Perhaps Christians should postpone their hopes of perfect love to the life of heaven. But it is hard to do so without setting a limit to what the Holy Spirit can do in the life of a man or woman. And this Wesley refused to do. At the risk of encouraging Pharisaism, he commanded his followers to be 'on the stretch for holiness' (the phrase is Mary Bosanquet's). May it not be that unless a Christian sets his spiritual aims as high as heaven itself, he is not likely even to reach the heights accessible to him?

Wesley is charged, or credited, by Lecky with having saved England from revolution in the eighteenth and early nineteenth centuries. The men, that is, who might have been urged on by the pitiable condition of the new industrial proletariat and their own powers of leadership to change the structure of society by force, became Methodists instead, and the *ancien régime* was saved. If it is meant that the Methodists were so preoccupied with the thought of an eternal beatitude which far outweighed the discomforts of earth that they recommended patient resignation in the face of economic tyranny, when the statement is false. They did not expect to reach heaven at all unless they had shown a deep compassion with the afflicted, and done everything they could to relieve their affliction, for this was part of holiness, and 'without holiness no man shall see the Lord'. Wesley never spared himself in the efforts to remove the social evils of his time—slavery above all, but also smuggling, cruelty, the luxury of the few, ill-health, vagabondage. and much else besides. If it is meant that their experience of Christian fellowship in their own meetings and of peace in their own hearts induced them to put up with wrongs inflicted on themselves more equably than is consistent with normal human nature, then the statement is true, and those who think that there is no effective social change without violence will remain angry with Methodism.

Wesley was in most respects a Tory in politics and a strong monarchist. He certainly would not have tolerated in his followers any tendency towards violent revolution. Nor did he see that there could be no widespread or permanent improvement in the lot of the poorer classes without far-reaching social legislation, in default of a revolution. He still believed in the effectiveness of charity. But it is not reasonable to criticize him for not holding a theory of economics and politics which had not yet been invented. It is more important to notice that his doctrine of Perfect Love instilled an attitude to one's fellow men which, in conjunction with other forces, led in the end to just such an appraisal of the order of society as Wesley is charged with not making, and to a sustained effort to change it.

We return to pure, as distinct from applied, theology. Those who came near to Perfect Love, or actually received it, had (according to Wesley's teaching) traversed the greater part of the 'way to heaven'. When they passed through the experience of physical death and appeared before the 'Great Assize', they would give account of their deeds on earth; and the verdict upon them would be determined, not on the score of their faith, as the Antinomians claimed, but on the score of their works. It might seem that here at the last Wesley has introduced the idea of merit which he has so strenuously resisted at all other points; but he counters the appearance of this by pointing out that our good works are really the gift of God to us. If we do not do them, we are to blame, and deserve the punishment of hell which awaits us; if we do them, we have no credit, for 'it is God who works in us, both to will and to do of his good pleasure'. So we are saved by grace, at the last as at the first.

If we look back on the 'plan of salvation' as Wesley outlines it, it is at once clear that it presupposes a positive and permeative doctrine of the Holy Spirit. We cannot call it a distinctive or peculiar doctrine, for Wesley says little or nothing about the Holy Spirit which other theologians would not accept. But the Holy Spirit is the Person in the Trinity who has suffered most from neglect—not from misunderstanding or heresy, but from neglect. Anyone who wishes to write a treatise on the Holy Spirit has far less literature to get through than those who attempt treatises on other theological subjects. Perhaps it is because of this that numerous Christian sects have made much play with the doctrine of the Holy Spirit without reasoned correction, though not without condemnation, from more orthodox thinkers. Wesley brings the doctrine of the Holy Spirit to life, and makes it strikingly concrete. To him, it is the Holy Spirit who converts the sinner and regenerates him; it is the Holy Spirit who witnesses to his spirit that he is a child of God; it is the Holy Spirit who enables and assists the believer's growth in holiness and brings him by stages to Perfect Love. The fellowship which he enjoys with his brethren is fellowship in the Holy Spirit, that is, a common sharing in the life and power which spring from Him. And, of course, in Wesley's eyes the Methodist Revival itself, and its astonishing growth, are the work of the Holy Spirit, not of any human agency; this is its only and sufficient justification.

But the emphasis on the Holy Spirit did not, with Wesley, mean any disparagement of the Church and its sacraments. The phrase 'High Churchman' did not, of course, in the eighteenth century bear the connotation which it now has, for the Oxford Movement had not taken place. But in the eighteenth-century sense, John Wesley, and perhaps still more his brother Charles, was a High Churchman. It is already clear that this is what he was in his early years. But to the end of his life he regarded the Church of England as the best-ordered Church in Christendom; he held that it was necessary for every Christian to avail himself of the ministrations of the Church, and in particular to attend 'the means of grace', and most of all to receive the Sacrament of Holy Communion; one of the most conspicuous signs of the Revival was the enormously increased attendance at Holy Communion in the Parish Church in those areas where Methodism had gained a strong foothold. Wesley did not publish any theology of the Eucharist (nor, perhaps, did he use the name), no doubt because he regarded the Anglican formularies as adequate. But he did encourage the publication, in the same volume with his brother's eucharistic hymns, of extracts from Daniel Brevint's *The Christian Sacrament and Sacrifice*. And Brevint, while repudiating transubstantiation, lays very strong emphasis on the Real Presence of Christ in the Sacrament, and makes frequent use of Christ's expressions about eternal Priesthood.

Wesley was also most explicit in his opposition to schism, both in the form of disunity of heart among those in the same communion, and still more in the form of actual separation. Such separation is permissible only when it is impossible to remain within a Church without committing a breach of God's commands or omitting something which He enjoins. But this kind of catholicity went together with another kind. In his pre-Aldersgate days, Wesley had had no truck with Dissenters, though he greatly valued the Moravians; later he learned a wider charity, and in his famous sermon on the 'Catholic Spirit' he urged unity with all Christians whose 'heart was right with God', who 'believed in Jesus Christ and walked by faith in Him'—even if their theology, their polity, and their liturgy did not conform with his own.

This is Wesley's theology of the 'way to heaven'—to be believed and preached not as if it were the totality of Christian faith, but within the firm framework of the Creeds. Wesley sometimes speaks to Methodists about 'our doctrines'; it is clear that he means by this those elements in the traditional Christian scheme which he believed to have been disregarded in contemporary theology and preaching, and therefore thought it particularly necessary to emphasize. He is making no claim to a special and distinctive doctrinal system. He refers on such occasions to the doctrines of salvation by faith, the witness of the Spirit, and Perfect Love; unless the Methodists preached these, he thought, there was no particular reason why they should preach at all; but it was their duty to preach the rest of the Christian Faith also.

John Wesley used every means open to his voice and pen for the propagation of his teaching. He preached and published his sermons; he wrote books and pamphlets and periodicals; he published abridged editions of theological works and sold them cheaply. If there had been any additional method of verbal communication he would certainly have used it. A selection of his sermons is still compulsory reading for those who wish to preach in Methodist Churches, and some of these, it is to be feared, make heavy weather of the task. Perhaps they have to read them at too early a stage of their intellectual development; for if and when a Methodist preacher reads them again in later years, he is astonished at their lucidity, cogency, orderliness, and depth. But the fact that they are difficult and troublesome to modern would-be theologians throws into relief the degree of theological literacy which Wesley expected of his apparently uneducated followers and assistants. It may be that people think and understand more clearly when their minds are directed along a few definite lines of interest than when they are subjected to a constant barrage of facts and theories on every subject from every quarter. Certainly Wesley's sermons would be hard going for a modern congregation.

Even more effective for Christian instruction than John Wesley's theological speaking and writing were Charles Wesley's hymns; and John made ample use of them for that reason. No doubt they also helped to stir up religious feelings and devout aspirations, and to knit together a large multitude into a worshipping community. But for John their main purpose was pedagogic, and if we had no sermons from his pen we should be able to reconstruct a passably accurate version of his theology from Charles Wesley's hymns.

He wrote more than six thousand—which is absurd. In this vast corpus there is a great deal which is banal, still more that is merely repetitive, and much employment of images which now strike us as grotesque. Even when the number has been reduced to a few hundred, by the exclusion of all that is ephemeral, extravagant, and flat, there is at least one metaphor which has to be deftly altered for the purposes of congregational singing. Charles has an unfortunate tendency to refer to members of the human race as 'worms', and the contemplation of our vermicular qualities sometimes leads him in strange directions. Without a smile, he was prepared to write, and congregations to sing, such lines as:

> And lift poor dying worms to heaven

or this, which places a particular strain on our conception of the animal world:

> And worms attempt to chant Thy praise.

But though Charles occasionally sinks to the depths, he more often rises to the heights, and having risen to them, he is capable of staying on them for a remarkably long time. Like other eighteenth century poets, he is a master of English Latinity. He has no particular desire to use an Anglo-Saxon word when one of Latin origin is available, and some of his most striking effects are achieved by the juxtaposition of a polysyllabic Latinism with a native word of simple meaning:

> That great mysterious Deity
> We soon with open face shall see:
> The beatific sight

Shall fill heaven's sounding courts with praise,
And wide diffuse the golden blaze
Of everlasting light.

The Father shining on His throne,
The glorious co-eternal Son,
The Spirit, one and seven,
Conspire our rapture to complete;
And lo! we fall before His feet,
And silence heightens heaven.

At other times he can be devastatingly simple:

Help us to help each other, Lord,
Each other's cross to bear,
Let each his friendly aid afford,
And feel his brother's care.

Help us to build each other up,
Our little stock improve;
Increase our faith, confirm our hope,
And perfect us in love.

He uses almost every metre known to man which can be set to a tune—including some which cause great difficulty to the musician:

O filial Deity
Accept my new-born cry;
See the travail of Thy soul,
Saviour, and be satisfied;
Take me now, possess me whole,
Who for me, for me hast died.

Yet some of his unusual metres are used to express with particular felicity the joy of liberation from fear and sin and the demands of a grasping conscience which is a characteristic of early Methodism:

Away with our fears,
Our troubles and tears;
The Spirit is come,
The witness of Jesus returned to His home.

And this one:

Captain of Israel's host, and Guide
Of all who seek the land above,

Beneath Thy shadow we abide,
The cloud of Thy protecting love:
Our strength, Thy grace; our rule, Thy word;
Our end, the glory of the Lord.

By Thine unerring Spirit led,
We shall not in the desert stray;
We shall not full direction need,
Nor miss our providential way;
As far from danger as from fear,
While love, almighty love, is near.

It is doubtful whether anyone could have compressed such large statements about divine grace and intimate human experience into the narrow limits of such constricting metres, unless he had received early training in the composition of Latin verse and been assisted by an exact knowledge of the Biblical text.

John and Charles Wesley published or sponsored four collections of hymns 'with tunes annexed' between 1742 and 1780. The tunes came from many sources. Some were written for the occasion by musical friends of Charles. Others were well-established psalm-tunes or German chorales. Others were adaptations of operatic tunes or borrowings of favourite airs; it is said that Charles was moved to write 'Love divine, all loves excelling', by hearing Purcell's melody to 'Fairest isle, all isles excelling', and the thought that such a tune deserved a worthier subject. The remark 'There is no reason why the Devil should have all the good tunes' is ascribed (in various forms) to Charles Wesley,* Rowland Hill (the Antinomian enemy of the Wesleys), and William Booth. The Devil had not extended his domain in this direction quite so far in Wesley's time as he has done since. But it is certainly true that Wesley did all he could to prevent him from doing so. Changes in musical taste have eliminated the majority of the tunes used by the Wesleys from modern hymn-books. But the reasons for exclusion have usually been the eighteenth century's tendency to undue floridity, not any cheapness or superficiality in the music. It was the later revivals of religion that stooped to ragtime.

John Wesley's definitive hymn-book was the 1780 *Collection of Hymns for the Use of the People called Methodists*, and for

* Charles certainly did write: 'Music, alas too long has been Press'd to obey the Devil' in one of his quainter poems.

this he wrote a preface which is reprinted in the present Methodist Hymn-book. In this he says of the book, which, of course, contains a large number of his brother's hymns, but also many from the pen of Isaac Watts, several of his own translations from the German, some metrical psalms, and a few hymns by other Methodist writers:

It is large enough to contain all the important truths of our most holy religion, whether speculative or practical; yea, to illustrate them all, and to prove them both by Scripture and reason; and this is done in a regular order.... So that this book is, in effect, a little body of experimental and practical divinity.

Of the book's aesthetic qualities he says:

In these hymns there is no doggerel; no botches; nothing put in to patch up the rhyme; no feeble expletives. Here is nothing turgid or bombast, on the one hand, or low and creeping, on the other. Here are no cant expressions; no words without meaning. Those who impute this to us know not what they say. We talk common-sense, both in prose and verse, and use no word but in a fixed and determinate sense.

But John Wesley was not concerned only with the words and their meaning. He issued very clear instructions in his hymn-book of 1770 as to how the hymns should be sung, as witness the following:

Sing *all*. See that you join with the congregation as frequently as you can. Let not a slight degree of weakness or weariness hinder you. If it be a cross to you, take it up, and you will find it a blessing.

Sing *lustily* and with a good courage. Beware of singing as if you were half-dead, or half-asleep; but lift up your voice with strength. Be not more afraid of your voice now, nor more ashamed of its being heard, than when you sang the songs of Satan.

Sing *modestly*. Do not bawl, so as to be heard above or distinct from the rest of the congregation, that you may not destroy the harmony; but survive to unite your voices together, so as to make one clear harmonious sound.

Sing *in Time*. Whatever tune is sung be sure to keep with it...

Above all sing *spiritually*. Have an eye to God in every word you sing. Aim at pleasing *Him* more than yourself, or any other creature. In order to do this attend strictly to the sense of what you sing, and see that your *Heart* is not carried away with the sound but offered to God continually; so shall your singing be such as the *Lord* will approve of here, and reward you when He cometh in the clouds of heaven.

Elementary instructions, perhaps, but not always observed.

Since the *Collection of Hymns* is intended as a vehicle of doctrine, the main part of it is divided into sections according to the various stages of the Christian life. Charles Wesley wrote his share of hymns for the great festivals of the Church, and covered in these the great Christological and Trinitarian themes. Best-known of Christmas hymns is what is now sung as:

Hark, the herald angels sing
Glory to the new-born King.*

But Charles wrote it thus:

Hark how all the welkin rings
  Glory to the king of Kings.

Rather less known is:

Let earth and heaven combine,
  Angels and men agree,
To praise in songs divine
  The incarnate Deity,
Our God contracted to a span
    Incomprehensibly made man.

For Easter there is 'Christ the Lord is risen today'; for Ascension 'Hail the day that sees Him rise'; for Whitsuntide 'Lord, we believe to us and ours'; for Trinity Sunday

Hail! Holy, holy, holy Lord
  Whom one in three we know;
By all Thy heavenly host adored,
  By all Thy Church below.

But the book was chiefly for the use of the Methodist Societies when they met by themselves for a preaching service or for Christian fellowship, and not for the services in the Parish Church, where music was otherwise provided for. So in the Wesley's *Collection* the 'introductory hymns' exhort sinners to return to God, and describe the pleasantness of religion, the goodness of God, and death, judgement, heaven, and hell. The first and second sections of the book proper contrast formal and

* It is sung every Christmas Eve in St Patrick's Cathedral, Dublin, not to the familiar tune, but to Handel's *Judas Maccabaeus*.

inward religion, and then provide hymns for repentant sinners. The main part of the book is then divided as follows. For believers rejoicing; fighting; praying; watching; working; suffering; seeking full redemption; saved; interceding for the world. Then comes a block of hymns for the intimate meetings of the Society, followed finally by a series of hymns on miscellaneous subjects, doctrinal and practical.

Here we see clearly the lineaments of John Wesley's theological scheme; and it is not an accident that by far the longest sub-sections are the two concerned with 'believers rejoicing' in the grace and mercy of God, and with 'believers seeking full redemption', that is, in quest of Scriptural holiness.

The invitations to sinners with which the *Collection* opens never fail to draw attention to the loving will of God:

> Sinners, turn, why will ye die?
> God, your Maker, asks you why;
> God, who did your being give,
> Made you with Himself to live;
> He the fatal cause demands,
> Asks the work of His own hands,
> Why, ye thankless creatures, why
> Will you cross His love, and die?

The 'mourner convinced of sin' asks in wonder:

> With glorious clouds encompassed round,
>   Whom angels dimly see,
> Will the Unsearchable be found,
>   Or God appear to me?
> Will He forsake His throne above,
>   Himself to worms impart?
> Answer, thou Man of grief and Love,
>   And speak it to my heart.

But it is the grace of God that brings out the most deeply-felt conviction:

> Jesus, my all in all Thou art;
>   My rest in toil; my ease in pain;
> The medicine of my broken heart;
>   In war my peace; in loss my gain;
> My smile beneath the tyrant's frown;
> In shame, my glory and my crown.

And this, in adoration:

Thee the first-born sons of light,
  In choral symphonies,
Praise by day, day without night,
  And never, never cease;
Angels and archangels, all
  Praise the mystic Three in One;
Sing, and stop, and gaze, and fall
  O'erwhelmed before Thy throne.

And this, in conscious reference, probably, to those who restricted the love of God to the predestined few:

Thy goodness and Thy grace to me,
  To every soul abound;
A vast, unfathomable sea,
  Where all our thoughts are drowned.

In streams the whole creation reach,
  So plenteous is the store:
Enough for all, enough for each,
  Enough for evermore.

The forgiven, regenerated, converted sinner must seek at once the gift of holiness:

Open, Lord, my inward ear
    And bid my heart rejoice;
Bid my quiet spirit hear
    Thy comfortable voice;
  Never in the whirlwind found,
Or where earthquakes rock the place,
  Still and silent is the sound,
    The whisper of Thy grace.

Show me, as my soul can bear,
    The depth of inbred sin;
All the unbelief declare,
    The pride that lurks within:
  Take me, whom Thyself hast bought;
Bring into captivity
  Every high aspiring thought,
    That would not stoop to Thee.

Or he may use these words:

Saviour from sin, I wait to prove
  That Jesus is Thy healing name;
To lose, when perfected in love,
  Whate'er I have, or can, or am:

I stay me on Thy faithful word :
'The servant shall be as his Lord.'

For Perfect Love is not an impossible ideal. And this is the real import of a hymn sung by many congregations without a glimmering of its meaning :

Love divine, all loves excelling,
Joy of heaven, to earth come down.
Fix in us Thy humble dwelling,
All Thy faithful mercies crown :
Jesus, Thou art all compassion :
Pure, unbounded love Thou art :
Visit us with Thy salvation :
Enter every trembling heart.

Finish, then, Thy new creation,
Pure and spotless let us be :
Let us see Thy great salvation,
Perfectly restored in Thee :
Changed from glory into glory,
Till in heaven we take our place,
Till we cast our crowns before Thee,
Lost in wonder, love and praise.

The 'great salvation' is Perfect Love, which God may grant us in this life.

The distinctively Methodist 'means of grace' for the pursuit of holiness was the fellowship of the Class Meeting, in which all the members knew themselves to belong to each other as well as Christ. Naturally there are many hymns provided for the devotional exercises of these small groups, and of the whole Society when it met as a united assembly of the Classes :

Jesus, united by Thy grace,
And each to each endeared,
With confidence we seek Thy face,
And know our prayer is heard.

Touched by the loadstone of Thy love,
Let all our hearts agree;
And ever towards each other move,
And ever move towards Thee.

But these Classes were always thought of as part of the great Church of Jesus Christ, and the unity and divine endowment of the Church were frequently in Charles Wesley's mind :

Christ, from whom all blessings flow,
  Perfecting the saints below,
Hear us, who Thy nature share,
  Who Thy mystic body are.

Love, like death, hath all destroyed,
  Rendered all distinctions void,
Names, and sects, and parties fall:
  Thou, O Christ, are all in all.

The sacramental hymns express a notably 'high' doctrine of the Lord's Supper:

Victim divine, Thy grace we claim,
  While thus Thy precious death we show:
Once offered up, a spotless lamb
  In Thy great temple here below,
Thou didst for all mankind atone,
And standest now before the throne.

We need not now go up to heaven,
  To bring the long-sought Saviour down;
Thou art to all already given,
  Thou dost even now Thy banquet crown:
To every faithful soul appear,
And show Thy real presence here.

And this expresses one essential element in the Christian's approach to the Lord's Table:

    Saviour, and can it be
    That Thou shouldst dwell with me?
From Thy high and lofty throne,
  Throne of everlasting bliss,
Will Thy majesty stoop down
  To so mean a house as this?

    I am not worthy, Lord,
    So foul, so self-abhorred,
Thee, my God, to entertain
  In my poor polluted heart:
I a frail and sinful man:
  All my nature cries: Depart!

    Yet come, Thou heavenly guest...

All British Christians would claim that they know Charles Wesley's hymns, since a selection of them has appeared in almost every Protestant hymn-book in the English language published since his time; and even those whose only acquaintance with Christianity comes from singing hymns at football matches know at least 'Jesus, lover of my soul'. But it is a curious fact that many of his hymns which Methodists most treasure, and which certainly take rank among his greatest, are not to be found in non-Methodist books—not even this one:

My heart is full of Christ, and longs
  Its glorious matter to declare.
Of Him I make my loftier songs,
  I cannot from His praise forbear;
My ready tongue makes haste to sing
  The glories of my heavenly king

Fairer than all the earth-born race,
  Perfect in comeliness Thou art:
Replenished are Thy lips with grace,
  And full of love Thy tender heart:
God ever blest! We bow the knee
  And own all fullness dwells in Thee.

Some of them are, no doubt, too intimate for public worship, and more suitable for private meditation. Others employ an idiom—though usually a Biblical one—which is familiar to Methodists from long use, but remote from other people's way of thinking. But the words, addressed to Methodists, of a Congregational scholar, Bernard L. Manning, deserve the attention of Christians in general:

> Your greatest—incomparably your greatest—contribution to the common heritage of Christendom is in Wesley's hymns. All the other things which you do, others have done and can do as well, better, or less well. But in Wesley's hymns you have something unique, no one else could have done it, and unless you preserve it for the use of all the faithful, till that day when we are all one, we shall all lose some of the best gifts of God.

If this sounds extravagant, it is at least true that the spirit of early Methodism is discernible more clearly in the hymns than anywhere else. The *Methodist Hymn Book* has been frequently revised, and more recently a Supplement, called *Hymns and Songs*, and containing much good modern material, has been published. Yet Charles Wesley's hymns remain essential to Methodist worship.

CHAPTER SIX

Anglicans and Methodists

In the light of what has now been recorded, it is perhaps not difficult to see why the Methodists fell out with their fellow-Anglicans. It was not about doctrine. Nothing that Wesley taught was at variance with the formularies of the Church of England, nor did he ever wish to question any of its doctrines. In a contest of orthodoxy with the prevailing school of thought among the bishops at any stage of his ministry, there is little doubt that he would have come off best. It is true that he laid more emphasis on the doctrine of salvation by faith than most of the clergy thought proper; but it was they, and not he, who were running counter to the *Article* and the *Homilies*. No doubt on such matters as the Witness of the Spirit and Perfect Love he could be said to be pushing certain elements in received doctrine to an unjustifiable extreme, and in the Church of England extreme forms even of her own doctrines are not welcome; but all that he said on these topics was well within the wide limits which she customarily allows to her clergy.

Nor was the constitution of the Methodist Societies in any way subversive of Anglican order. The Societies were never, of course, registered with the Anglican authorities and accepted by them as part of the framework of the Church of England. But that was not the sort of thing that happened in the eighteenth century. The Societies were nevertheless within the Church of England, and threatened neither to disrupt nor to depart from it. There were many other Religious Societies, as we have seen, and they were not regarded as schismatic. Methodism, in its nation-wide development, did not exactly fall into line with these much more inward-looking religious groups; it had affinities with them, but also with the great evangelistic societies, the Society for the Propagation of the Gospel and the Society for the Promotion of Christian Knowledge. But there was nothing here to incur the suspicion of sectarianism or to lead to a breach.

It was the methods used by Wesley and his friends to expand the Societies that were offensive. In spite of his own natural predilection for established order, Wesley felt himself obliged by the necessity of the Gospel not only to preach in the open air, but also to do so in other men's parishes without invitation or permission. He was careful never to do so at the time of the statutory services in the Parish Church, and he persistently urged his followers to attend all such services, including Holy Communion above all. But to gather round him a vast crowd of people who had for the most part never been seen in Church, to have them singing noisy hymns, to produce outbursts of religious fervour such as the neighbourhood had never seen before, to organize those affected in this way into Societies which met in large numbers every week, to preach things which sounded dangerously near the suggestion that Jack is as good as his master (for did he not teach that God loved master and man alike?)—and to do all this without permission under the very nose of the man who was responsible for the souls of all who lived in the parish—was this not rank '*enthusiasm*'? It is easy to see how devout parish priests who faithfully carried out their cure of souls and the others who spent their time drinking and gaming with the squire were equally incensed.

Nor, whatever Wesley might say, did the temper of the newly-converted Methodists always help to endear the movement to the bishops and clergy. Some of them, no doubt, were Dissenters in origin, and had no love at all for the Church which had persecuted their fathers and was guilty of many deviations from Christian truth. But there were not many of these, and they did not much affect the situation. More significant in this regard is the fact that many of the converts, though nominally Anglican, had never received any real care from the Church of England since their baptism, partly, no doubt, by their own and their parents' fault, but largely because of the inadequacy of the Anglican organization to deal with the population in the growing industrial areas. They owed their souls, as they would have said, to the preaching of the Methodists; they did not feel any particular loyalty to the Church which had neglected them. No doubt, too, many of them were brash and self-confident, as new converts are apt to be, and had no compunction about pointing out, directly and indirectly, the failings of the official pastors and the spiritual supineness of their flocks. Unless there was exceptional wisdom on both sides, personal relations between Anglicans and Methodists, especially in small towns and villages, were apt to deteriorate.

The response to all this of the average incumbent and his leading laymen was not particularly constructive. It often took the form of undisguised contempt for the illiterate, ill-regulated religious upstarts that the Methodists were taken to be. It showed itself very frequently in petty persecutions and small personal affronts. And when the Methodists built for themselves more and more preaching-places for the purposes of their own devotions outside Church hours, it found a convenient legal outlet. By the Act of Toleration of 1689 it was permissible to build and attend chapels for non-Anglican worship, provided that (*a*) the teaching there given was not Roman Catholic or anti-Trinitarian, and (*b*) the building was registered with the proper authorities as a Dissenting Chapel. When the Methodist buildings began to go up, the law was technically infringed, but only technically, it might be thought, since the buildings belonged to a Society which professed allegiance to Anglican principles. Wesley therefore did not think it necessary to register them. But his opponents saw an opportunity of discomfiting him, and threatened prosecution in many places if the law was not complied with. Wesley was indeed discomfited: for if he registered the chapels, he would have to register them as Dissenting Chapels, and he entirely repudiated the notion that Methodists were Dissenters. The Act of Toleration also required those who wished to preach outside the confines of the Established Church to register themselves as Dissenting Preachers; and Wesley was naturally quite unwilling that his preachers should be thus registered. So the anti-Methodists could threaten the preachers with prosecution also—and sometimes get them pressed into the army. In the end Wesley had to give way on both these points, though it was not until 1787 that he formally advised all chapels and preachers to be licensed—and at the same time insisted that the Chapels should be called Methodist Chapels and the preachers 'preachers of the Gospel' everywhere except in the actual legal documents.

From the first moment until the last of Wesley's itinerant ministry the authorities of the Church of England did precisely nothing, either to prevent a breach or to expel the Methodists. Individual bishops from time to time acted in their own diocese in ways that showed that they approved or disapproved of what the Methodists were doing. But of concerted official action there was nothing. From one point of view, there could not be any, for the Convocations did not meet. But there was not even what presumably there could have been, some kind of informal consultation on the subject between the bishops. Still less, after the interview between Wesley and the Bishop of Bristol in 1739, was there any discussion of Methodist proceedings between Wesley and any official spokesman of the Church of England, though sometimes Wesley met a bishop in a social way, and even had dinner with Bishop Lavington of Exeter, his old vitriolic opponent. In such a situation as this, every man acted as his own adviser.

John Wesley's own position was quite clear. He intended to carry out his mission 'to spread Scriptural Holiness throughout the land' by means which he believed to be wholly consistent with the doctrines and practices of the Church of England; he had no intention of separating himself from that Church, of which he professed himself a completely loyal member until his dying day. Whenever his helpers raised the question of separation, as they did from time to time, he instantly forbade all thought of it. Yet it was his own actions, more than any other single factor, that precipitated the division which ultimately took place.

In 1746, while he was riding from London to Bristol, he read an early work, written in 1691, of Peter King, a Puritan who ultimately became Lord Chancellor, called *Account of the Primitive Church*. This book seemed to Wesley to demonstrate first that in the New Testament bishops and presbyters constitute the same order (King added that bishops were higher in *degree*, but Wesley did not take particular note of this point); secondly that therefore presbyters as well as bishops have the right to ordain; and thirdly that during the first three hundred years of the Christian era presbyters did from time to time ordain. We know from a letter written by John and Charles Wesley together a few weeks earlier that until he read King's treatise John was convinced that 'the three-fold order of ministers is not only authorized by its apostolical institutions, but also by the Written Word'. But King's arguments completely convinced him of the error of this view and for the rest of his life he never departed from King's position.

He was confirmed in it by Edward Stillingfleet's *Irenicum*. Stillingfleet wrote this when he was twenty-four, in 1659, and perhaps never repudiated its main contentions, when he became Bishop of Worcester. He showed that no particular form of Church government is laid down in Scripture, and that therefore neither Episcopacy nor Presbyterianism can claim to be of divine right. Wesley was persuaded by this that although the government of the Church of England was admirable and scripturally carried out, yet other forms of Church government were legitimate, and might in fact be ordained by the Holy Spirit in particular circumstances.

But although Wesley was certain of the soundness of King's argument, he refused to act on it for thirty-eight years. His love for the Church of England, and his desire to avoid all forms of strife, were so strong that he resolutely turned away from any temptation to forward his work by ordaining his own preachers or allowing his followers to hold services in Church times. It is probable that he regarded himself as 'Superintendent' of the Methodists, and he was well aware that 'superintendent' was only a latinized form of 'bishop'. But he carried this no further.

Until 1784. In that year he took two drastic steps, each, as he thought, under the pressure of evangelical necessity. He had been concerned for a long time, of course, about the future of the work which he had begun, and he was now eighty-one years old. The man he had wished to designate as his successor, Fletcher of Madeley, was in very poor health (he died in the next year). There was no hope at all that the authorities of the Church of England would take up and further the work of Methodism (many of them were surely hoping that it would peter out when the old man died). He could not see among his followers anyone sufficiently outstanding to be worthy of the full task of leadership. He therefore, by a legal 'Deed of Declaration' lodged in the Court of Chancery, appointed a Conference of a hundred specified men, and made that Conference his successor, with power to fill up its ranks as death diminished them. This body was always thereafter known as the 'Legal Hundred'. Thus he formed the Methodist Societies into an *ecclesiola in ecclesia*, and gave it a concretely historical existence and constitution.

By 1784 the American War of Independence was over, and

the Americans were free. The Anglican clergyman who were working in the country when the war broke out had—naturally enough—supported the British cause. They ceased to be welcome to the Americans, and came back to England. Wesley's American preachers had been careful in most cases to remain neutral in the struggle, and some had openly backed the American side. They were therefore welcome in the new America. But none of them was ordained, with the unfortunate result that it was scarcely possible to receive Holy Communion from a duly authorized person in the whole of the United States. This was in Wesley's mind an appalling situation, and he could see no sign that the Bishop of London, in whose diocese America was, was taking steps to remedy it. Wesley had introduced a Methodist preacher to the Bishop in 1780, and had asked him to ordain him. The Bishop had refused, officially on the ground that the clergy on the spot in America could cope with the situation (there *were* a few of them). Wesley took this as an indication of the Bishop's intention to do nothing, and nothing ever happened to dispel this impression. Samuel Seabury, elected bishop by his fellow-clergy in Connecticut, had come over to England in 1783 in order to be consecrated. The Archbishop of York (there was a vacancy at Canterbury at the time) refused to consecrate him, on the ground that the law required an oath of allegiance to the English Crown from anyone to be consecrated bishop, and that only a special Act of Parliament could dispense with this requirement. We cannot tell if Wesley was aware of this, but if he was it must have strengthened his conviction that the English bishops were prepared to do exactly nothing to deal with a desperate situation. So at last, early in the morning of 1 September 1784, at 6 Dighton Street, Bristol, without consulting his Conference, he ordained Richard Whatcoat and Thomas Vasey as deacons. On the following day he ordained them presbyters, and on the same occasion consecrated the Rev. Thomas Coke, who was episcopally ordained, as Superintendent. The three men shortly afterwards set out for America, and we shall later have to record their doings in the building up of Methodism in that country. By one of the ironies of history, Samuel Seabury was consecrated bishop at Aberdeen by the Bishop of Brechin and two other Scottish Bishops (the oath of allegiance not being required by them) on 14 November in the same year. But Wesley could have known nothing of the discussions which preceded this event, nor did he have any reason to suspect that it would happen.

The doctrine of the ministry on which John Wesley acted was no doubt a permissible one in the Church of England; but to act on it was to flout the laws and discipline of that Church. Charles Wesley saw this clearly, and deplored it bitterly, maintaining that 'ordination was separation'. John, with an obtuseness that was not characteristic of him, refused to acknowledge this, and continued to argue against separation for the rest of his life.

Only an act of farsighted statesmanship could now have retained the Methodists in the Anglican communion (or brought them back to it, according to the way Wesley's ordinations are looked at). This was not forthcoming. Perhaps none of the bishops heard about the event in Dighton Street; but if they had all heard about it, it is very doubtful whether they would have done anything about it. Wesley, having crossed the Rubicon, advanced further into the forbidden territory. He ordained presbyters for Scotland and for the mission field in 1785 and 1786. And in 1788 and 1789 he ordained a few men for work in parts of England where the Methodists could not obtain the Sacrament, and consecrated one man Superintendent. In 1786 the Conference allowed Methodist services to be held at Church times in parishes where the minister was notoriously wicked or heretical, where there were not enough churches to contain half the population, or where there was no church within two miles.

After John Wesley's death in 1791, the separation was soon consummated. Many of the Methodist Societies were painfully divided within themselves until 1795 on the question whether the Methodist preachers, not ordained episcopally, should give them the Sacrament of Holy Communion. Those members who had been appointed as Trustees of the property (mostly by Wesley himself) sturdily maintained that they should not, and went so far as to bar from their pulpits (as they were legally entitled to do) any preachers who had given the Sacrament. The rest of the members tended to take the other view. They could not see why the men who ministered to them in all other spiritual matters should not minister to them in this one too. The Conference therefore had to deal each year with disputes liable to lead to a split in the whole body of Methodists. In 1793 it was agreed that when a Society unanimously wished for the Sacrament from a Methodist preacher it should receive it. This did not restore peace, and in the next year the Conference allowed the preachers to administer the Sacrament wherever union and concord could not be preserved without it. But a pamphlet war still raged, and in 1795 a compromise, known as the 'Plan of Pacification', was accepted by almost all: it provided that if the Sacrament was desired by a majority of the Trustees and of the Class Leaders, meeting separately, it should be given. The option allowed by the Plan was taken up quickly by all the Societies that wished to remain in association with the Conference, and by the end of the eighteenth century the Methodist Church had come into organized and permanent existence. The Conference of 1793 did, however, leave open one way back. It ruled that ordination of Methodist preachers should not take place by the laying on of hands, but should be by 'reception into full connexion' with the Conference—that is, by a formal vote of the Conference, accompanied by prayer. It was thought by those who did not want to break all links with the Church of England that subsequent re-union would be easier if Methodist preachers had not had hands laid upon them. This enactment remained in force for Britain until 1836.

The series of events which culminated in the final separation of the Methodists from the Church of England must always remain a subject for fierce discussion. The various degrees of blame incurred must be left to the decision of the Last Judgement. Meanwhile it can fairly be said that the choice facing first of all John Wesley, and after his death the Methodist Conference, was this: is the work of spreading Scriptural holiness assigned by God to the Methodists to be continued, in defiance of the laws of the Church of England, at the cost in the last resort of separation from her? Or are her laws to be kept and separation avoided, at the cost of stopping this work of God? This was a harsh dilemma, and the first requirement of those who wish to heal the breach between Anglicans and Methodists is that they should recognize how harsh it was.

CHAPTER SEVEN

Nineteenth-century Vicissitudes

In the perspective of history, the final separation of the Methodists from the Church of England happened very quickly. But the speed was not great enough for the Methodists who felt themselves most remote from the sober and solemn (and, as they thought, sluggish and corrupt) ways of the mother Church. These men found a leader in Alexander Kilham (1762–98). He was a fiery and effective preacher, and at heart at least as much a Dissenter as a Methodist. In the period of confusion before the Plan of Pacification, he disseminated pamphlets which fiercely urged the rights of the Trustees of Methodist buildings to ask whom they willed to administer the Sacraments, whatever the Class Leaders and members might do or say. Also, in his view, a clearly Congregationalist one, the Society in each place had complete powers of discipline—a view which he did not altogether succeed in reconciling with his conviction about the authority of Trustees. In fact, it looks rather as if he was willing to use any stick which came to hand for beating those who opposed rapid separation from the Church of England. The Plan of Pacification did not pacify him. With six other preachers he refused to sign it, and continued a violent propaganda campaign in favour of giving the Trustees the absolute right in the matter of the Sacrament. When he disobeyed an instruction to call a halt to his operations, he was excluded from the list of preachers. William Thom, one of the six other dissidents, followed him out by resigning, and the two of them founded the Methodist New Connexion in 1797, with a membership of about 5,000. Thom, a much more reasonable man than Kilham, became the first President of the New Connexion's Conference, with Kilham as Secretary. In 1798 Kilham died, having burnt himself out in evangelism and agitation. But the New Connexion survived and grew, with a constitution very similar to that of the main body of Methodists, except that it gave far more powers to the laity.

All this was a shock, but not a very profound one, to the Conference which had succeeded Wesley as the controlling influence in Methodism. The development of Methodism went steadily on. The real effects of the decisive break with the Church of England were to some extent concealed for the time being. The preachers forbore for thirty years to call themselves 'ministers'; they were just 'preachers of the Gospel'. Marriages, funerals, and often baptisms of Methodists still took place in the Parish Church. The Societies opted for their own celebration of Holy Communion one by one, not all in a body. Yet during this period of adjustment the Methodist Societies found, partly to their own surprise, and certainly to the surprise of their critics, who had hoped that the death of Wesley was the beginning of the end of Methodism, that they possessed all that was needed to constitute an independent Church; all that was needed, that is, according to Wesley's and their own theology, though not according to the received Church order of the Church of England. They had the Gospel, the Sacraments, the pursuit of Christian holiness, the Scriptures, preachers and pastors, a closely-knit organization for the Connexion at large and for the individual Societies, enough chapels for their purposes, and the resources to build more. All that they lacked was episcopal succession; and they felt that they could dispense with that, though many of them sadly missed the decency and dignity which went with it inside the Church of their fathers. Methodism was now a Church as well as a Society, and so it has remained. And to Church order and Church organization was steadily added a Church consciousness which grew with every year of the nineteenth century.

But with these very desirable possessions went another which was not so desirable—bourgeois respectability. Even in Wesley's time, as we have seen, the Methodists, by their thrift, industry, and sobriety, had become economically comfortable; and the religion of the economically comfortable tends to develop certain characteristics—a confusion of social with spiritual and moral status, a complacency with the way in which things are done in *our* chapel, an unwillingness to sanction teaching which may disrupt the existing social order, and (very curious in Methodists) a fear of any emotion which does not follow the exact lines laid down by ecclesiastical authority.

We have to remember, too, that the early years of the

nineteenth century were years of national fear and sometimes panic. Napoleon was still at large for a decade and a half; and the other forces unleashed by the French Revolution were just as dangerous and more persistent. The Combination Acts of the turn of the century show the mood of desperate self-preservation which actuated the ruling classes. The Luddite and Radical agitations, culminating in the 'massacre' of Peterloo (strikingly similar to the Sharpeville shootings of 1959 in motive, nature and results), led up to the repressive Six Acts of 1820. But these did not dam the incoming tide of democratic reform, and the established classes of England trembled in their shoes many times more before the Reform Act of 1832 produced a temporary settlement.

Fifty years earlier, the Methodists might have wished to find themselves enrolled among the rebels—though Wesley would not have allowed it to happen. Now their temper was very different. They wished to preserve the place in the social order which they had so painfully won, and they wished the social order in which they had found that place to be preserved at all costs. They knew themselves to be still suspected—quite unjustly—of subversionary tendencies. In 1800 the Bishop of Rochester had stated that sedition and atheism were the real objects of their institutions. In 1810 a clergyman J.P. in Bath was still saying that the rapid progress being made by the Methodists must tend to the subversion of order. So the Conference almost fell over backwards in the effort to make it clear that it had no truck with Radical or any other kind of agitators, and published annually a protestation of deep loyalty to the Crown and an instruction to the Methodist people to abstain from political activity. Methodism had became middle-class conservative.

But there were some in whom the old rebellious spirit still smouldered and could be roused to a flame. The activities of Hugh Bourne (1772–1852) and William Clowes (1780–1851) appealed to them at once. Bourne was born on a farmstead near Stoke-on-Trent and became a carpenter; he acquired an extensive education, including the knowledge of Greek, Hebrew, Latin, and French, entirely by his own efforts. The religious perplexities of his youth were resolved partly by some Quaker literature, but more by John Fletcher's writings, and so he became a Methodist, though he sometimes showed signs of the early Quaker influence. In the fashion of the Methodist pioneers, once he was 'converted' himself he began to convert others. At Harriseahead, in the neighbourhood of Tunstall, he formed a society and built a chapel, in the year of 1800. He had no authority or permission to do such things, and he was not even an officially accredited 'local preacher', but the value of his work was recognized, and his chapel was included in the Tunstall Circuit by Conference action. But he was not content to act on the conventional lines of Methodist preachers. He had heard of religious gatherings called 'Camp Meetings' which were being held with great *élan* in America, and planned to imitate them. It seems that large companies of people assembled in an out-of-the-way place, with provisions and improvised camping equipment. Then they settled down to a prayer meeting, interspersed with 'revival addresses', for a day and a night and a day, and sometimes longer, with short intervals for sleeping and eating. Reports of these meetings reached England in various forms, many of them, no doubt, garbled. Bourne was much impressed, and when Lorenzo Dow, one of the organizers of this kind of revival, started preaching in England, he immediately invited his assistance. As a result the first English 'Camp Meeting' took place on Mow Cop (a hill not chosen for its scenic beauty) on 31 May 1807.

Now this was just the sort of thing that the Conference was afraid of. In the first place, many of the reports of American Camp Meetings had told of violent emotionalism, not unmixed with sexual licence; in the second place, large gatherings of people (something between 2,000 and 4,000 people were said to have been present) in secluded spots were bound to be suspected of sedition. Bourne was, of course, quite innocent of any attempt at subversion and would have dealt severely with any licence. But the Conference—without, perhaps, making any very careful investigation—forthwith forbade 'Camp Meetings'. Bourne was compelled by his conscience to go on with them, and in 1808 was expelled from membership in the Tunstall Circuit on the curious but convenient charge of absenting himself from the Class Meeting. Soon afterwards, not very far away in Burslem, Clowes, who had been a speaker at the first Camp Meeting, and had since then been organizing his own, was expelled from membership for flouting the rules of the Conference. Bourne and Clowes joined forces, and in 1810 formed the Society of Primitive Methodists.

Clowes seems to have taken this step with great reluctance; Bourne was, perhaps, of a more sectarian temper. The two men shared the leadership of the new Society, but the actual responsibility of administration fell more and more on Bourne, who was one of the genuine, rugged leaders of men that the English countryside from time to time produces, tireless in mind and body, eloquent, and astonishingly gifted in literary and organizing ability. When he died, the Primitive Methodist Society numbered 110,000 members and mustered 560 travelling preachers.

Even their prompt repudiation of errant revivalism did not save the Wesleyan Methodists (as the members of the parent body were now called) from Government suspicion; after all, they could hardly expect the authorities of the country to make nice distinctions between brands of illiterate dissidents. In fact, it was the alleged illiteracy of Methodists that in 1811 gave Lord Sidmouth, Home Secretary in Lord Liverpool's Government, the excuse to bring in a Bill to ban Methodist preachers, both itinerant and local. The Bill was theoretically designed to raise the intellectual qualifications of all preachers outside the Established Church, but the qualifications were carefully stated in such a way as to admit the exponents of recognized Dissent, but to disallow the Methodists, who had not yet reached the same academic standard as the Congregationlists and Baptists. The real motive of the whole affair was the panic fear of rebellion. The Conference had fortunately set up a decade previously a 'Committee of Privileges' to defend the civil rights of Methodists. The Committee succeeded in allaying Lord Sidmouth's suspicions, and he dropped the Bill. The Lords, even more zealous for the preservation of public order and themselves, wished to push it through, but the Archbishop of Canterbury, Manners-Sutton, took a larger view, and persuaded them to drop it, on the ground that it was a breach of the Act of Toleration. Soon afterwards the belated repeal of the Conventicle and Five Mile Acts removed the last legal objections to the existence of the Methodist Societies—and showed that English statesmen were at last thinking in terms of full religious liberty.

The crisis in Methodism which produced the Primitive Methodist separation was repeated in a slightly different form a little while after the Wesleyan Methodist Conference had reached a negotiated peace with the State. Once again it was brought about by a fervent preacher who could not keep the rules of official Methodism. William O'Bryan (1778–1868) was a Cornishman of Irish descent; his father was a wealthy farmer, and William received a very adequate education. After his conversion he became an enthusiastic local preacher in the neighbourhood of Newquay, but his zeal did not allow him to be local enough in his activities to satisfy Circuit and Conference regulations. Expelled from Methodist membership in 1810, he worked as a free-lance evangelist, and formed Societies in several areas which the Methodist preachers had not so far visited. In 1814 he was readmitted to the Methodist ranks, and his Societies were incorporated in the Methodist Connexion. But he was soon restive again, and a repetition of his zealous indiscipline led to a second expulsion. Once again on his own, he accepted the invitation of James Thorne, not a Methodist but an Anglican profoundly dissatisfied with the ministrations of his Church, to work in the village of Shebbear in North Devon. Here, in 1815, the Bible Christian Society was founded, and organized on Methodist lines, with O'Bryan as the first President of its Conference and James Thorne the first Secretary.

This was not, strictly, a Methodist schism, for, apart from O'Bryan himself, the first Bible Christians were not Methodists at all in the accepted sense. For the first years of the movement they operated in rural areas untouched by Wesleyan Methodists, and were careful not to compete with them in any way; though they spread eastwards as far as Bristol and the Isle of Wight, there was never any deliberate opposition. Yet if O'Bryan had been more amenable and the Wesleyan Conference more flexible, it would have been natural for the Bible Christian Societies to have become part of ordinary Methodism, to the great advantage of all. O'Bryan himself was no doubt a firebrand and an individualist: the Bible Christian Conference resisted his claims to be a perpetual President and decide all matters by his single vote, and he set off to found a new sect in America and Canada. But James Thorne was a balanced and catholic-spirited man, and under his guidance the new connexion advanced steadily in the West country. Its most notable, or notorious, achievements were the full authorization of women itinerant preachers (whom the men preachers were connexionally advised to marry), and the evangelistic exploits of Billy Bray (1794–1868), a converted drunkard and lecher, whose name is still to be conjured with in Cornish Nonconformity.

One of the reasons why the Wesleyan Methodists were not so troubled or conscience-stricken as they should have been by this and the earlier examples of separation, was the rapid growth of their Church. Only 72,000 strong in Britain at Wesley's death (though four times that number attended Methodist services) it had advanced by several thousand every year, and by 1820 had reached nearly 200,000. But in that year the first decrease since 1766 (when figures were first calculated) was reported to the Conference in Liverpool, and there was much consternation. It was felt that the reason for the decline was a lack of concentration on the supreme task of evangelism, and the following resolutions (among others) were passed, to be read annually to all Methodist preachers:

1. We, on this solemn occasion, devote ourselves afresh to God; and resolve, in humble dependence on His grace, to be more than ever attentive to personal religion, and to the Christian instruction and government of our own families.

2. Let us endeavour, in our public ministry, to preach constantly all those leading and vital doctrines of the Gospel, which peculiarly distinguished the original Methodist preachers, whose labours were so signally blessed by the Lord, and to preach them in our primitive method—evangelically, experimentally, zealously, and with great plainness and simplicity; giving to them a decided pre-eminence in every sermon, and labouring to apply them closely, affectionately, and energetically to the conscience of the different classes of our hearers.

3. Let us consecrate ourselves fully and entirely to our proper work as servants of Christ in His church, giving ourselves 'wholly' to it, both in public and in private, and guarding against all occupations of our time and thoughts which have no direct connexion with our great calling and which would injuriously divert our attention from the momentous task of saving souls, and taking care of the flock of Christ.

Many of the Resolutions were, of course, designed to improve the spiritual efficiency of the Methodist organization, but there is no exclusive concern with the affairs of one denomination. Fully in harmony with John Wesley's practice and precept is this 'ecumenical' Resolution:

12. Let us ourselves remember, and endeavour to impress on our people, that we as a Body do not exist for the purpose of party; and that we are especially bound by the example of our Founder, and by our constant professions before the world, to avoid a narrow, bigoted, and sectarian spirit.... Let us therefore maintain towards all denominations of Christians, who 'hold the Head', the kind and catholic spirit of primitive Methodism.

Wesleyan Methodism had certainly not yet fallen into the trap of denominational imperialism.

The carrying out of these Resolutions, combined, no doubt, with social factors, seems to have effectively checked the decrease in membership, and for nearly thirty years there was almost uninterrupted advance—an advance more than commensurate with the rapid growth of population in industrial England. The attitude of official Methodism to the world outside was now exclusively evangelistic, as the 'Liverpool Minutes' had enjoined; in face of the continued Radical agitation there was the same conscientious abstention from politics as before—it was even said by the Radicals that Methodist pulpits were used for commending the obnoxious Six Acts of 1820. But the veto on politics was not, of course, universally obeyed. The Wesleyan Methodists (as well as the other kinds of Methodist) were in many cases the very people whose political and economic grievances were the most pressing, and in such cases very often, because of long training in Class Meetings, the most articulate members of their social group; nothing that the Conference said could entirely prevent them from identifying themselves with their fellow-sufferers. Even the Conference did not forbid its members to join the Trade Unions, which became legal in 1824, and when the Reform agitation reached its climax between 1830 and 1832, Methodist preachers were often to be found urging the serious necessity of the Reform Bill, while at the same time, of course, reminding their hearers of the importance of moderation and restraint.

The passing of the Reform Bill into law seems to have persuaded the Wesleyan Methodist authorities that all injustices were now set right; at any rate, they turned back to their own affairs with some concentration—only to find that the kind of agitation which they so deplored in the world outside was now being directed against their own régime within their own Church. The period from 1830 to 1870 was a period of persistent agitation and of the painful and reluctant democratization of the Methodist constitution.

For most of these years the spirit of Methodism as Wesley was thought to have left it was embodied in one man, Jabez Bunting, and he became the target for the agitation, personal and political, which was intended to bring Methodism into greater accord with the temper of the times. Bunting was on any showing a remarkable personality, and it is only the fact that he was a conservative in an age of revolution that has prevented his recognition as one of the great ecclesiastical statesmen. Certainly, in intellectual ability, oratorical persuasiveness, and administrative foresight, though not, perhaps, in humility and willingness to learn from lesser men, he towered above his Methodist contemporaries. He was a Manchester man, and his first charge after ordination in 1803 was also in Manchester. Eleven years later he was Secretary of the Wesleyan Conference, and in 1820 President for the first of four terms of office. He held almost every high office in the Connexion in the course of his career; but his official status was as nothing compared with the personal influence and power that he enjoyed. ('Enjoyed' is probably the right word.) No President for thirty years could feel happy unless he had Bunting's advice and support, both during the Conference and for the year of office that followed. As early as 1828 a minister said of him: 'The whole Methodist Conference is buttoned up in a single pair of breeches.'

He showed his attitude to political radicalism in his early ministry: when, in 1812, a Luddite was shot while breaking into a mill in Cleckheaton, and elaborate preparations for his funeral were made by the local Methodists, Bunting refused to take the service. His views on this did not change. In 1827 he is reported to have said that Methodism was as opposed to democracy as it was to sin. His defenders have urged that he was nevertheless in favour of steady reform, and that even in Church matters he showed signs of wishing for a growth of cooperation between ministers and laity. But he held very firmly to the principle that the care and government of the Church belonged to the ordained ministry, and he rigorously opposed any alteration of the composition of the Conference to admit laymen. By the same token he upheld the supreme rights of the Superintendent Minister in his own Circuit.

The first signs of discontent appeared in 1827. The trustees of Brunswick Chapel, Leeds, had decided to put an organ in. This, in the judgement of many Methodists, was a dreadful thing to do. Like some of the Puritans of the seventeenth century, they thought that God wished the human voice in worship to be unassisted by any mechanical contrivance. This comparatively minor issue was soon swallowed up in a much larger one. The trustees were mostly successful Leeds business-men who had moved out from the city into more commodious residences. The people who attended the church, and their leaders, were against the organ. A Special District Meeting, of all the itinerant preachers in the District, voted to ban the organ. The trustees appealed to the Conference, and the Conference ruled against the District Meeting and sanctioned the organ. This was seen as the Conference setting itself up as Pope and oppressing the Methodist people. The result was the secession of the 'Protestant Methodists'.

This affair was chiefly local, but the feeling that the Conference, mainly in the person of Bunting, was trampling on the rights of the Methodist people spread rapidly during the next few years. It was vigorously fomented by James Everett, an able, eloquent, restless minister with a morosely mordant wit and a pungent pen, He was sincerely convinced that Bunting was eaten up with ambition, and he construed everything that Bunting did or said as fresh evidence for his conviction. It was proposed in the early thirties that an 'Institution' should be set up for the training of Methodist ministers—a harmless and useful proposal, one would have thought. Everett opposed it, not, as he was at pains to point out, because he had any 'objection to ministerial training in the abstract', but because 'the people were not consulted in the matter', and because: 'It was strongly suspected that the prime mover and promoter of the project was seeking to furnish himself with a pretext for quietly sitting down in London, the seat of Methodist government, for the remainder of his life, the place where he had been so long and acquired so much influence... The suspicion rested on the belief that his own ease, influence, honour, or power were generally mixed up, more or less, with all his great measures.' It is true that Bunting was to be appointed President of the 'Theological Institution', and no doubt everyone knew this; but Everett's suspiciousness seems almost neurotic.

As part of his campaign against the Institution, Everett wrote a pamphlet called *Disputants*, without attaching his name to to it, though he confessed his authorship five years later. This publication was the beginning of the internal warfare by anonymous pamphlet which was to do grievous harm to Methodism during the next two decades. Everett next brought out a volume called *Wesleyan Takings* (written by himself and another minister called Crowther, as he afterwards acknowledged), which contained satirical sketches of Bunting and his principal henchmen. It was aimed against 'centralization and usurped power', and the 'plans, partialities, and usurpations of Dr Bunting and his nominees' (to quote Everett's own words). There was a hue-and-cry for the authors, and several ministers were at first suspected. But suspicion soon narrowed itself down to Everett and an associate of his called Burdsall, and they were sternly reprimanded by the Conference, not for the authorship, which was not proved, but for the refusal to deny authorship, which was.

Everett kept the peace for a while after this, but in 1846, 1847 and 1848 appeared four more anonymous pamphlets, called *Fly Sheets*, containing more venom than anything so far, though their accusations of tyranny, undue centralization, and misuse of Connexional money were now familiar. This time the 'body' (Wesleyan Methodism's curious name for itself in the nineteenth century) was set by the ears. Everett's agitation had not entirely failed in its effect; there were many 'democratic' Methodists up and down the country who were sure that the 'dominant party' ruled the Church autocratically and badly. The Conference seems to have got into something like a panic when every known means of discovering the authorship of the *Fly Sheets* had failed. Every minister was requested to sign a document declaring his detestation of the sentiments contained in the *Sheets*, and those who, after two repetitions of the request, refused to do so, were required to appear before the Conference of 1849. Everett was among them, and was the first to be asked the question: 'Are you the author of the *Fly Sheets*?' He refused to reply. So did five others, including Samuel Dunn and William Griffith, who said that they would reply only if they were allowed to explain their answers. The Conference thereupon decided to expel Everett for contumacy, and Dunn and Griffith because they declined to promise to discontinue their articles for the *Wesleyan Times* and the *Wesley Banner*, periodicals which had spread Everett's views. The others were censured.

The expected result took place. Everett was too powerful a man to retire at this point into private life. He formed the 'Wesleyan Reform Society', and united this in 1857 with the 'Wesleyan Methodist Association'. This had been formed by an amalgamation of the Protestant Methodists with the followers of Samuel Warren, who had led the opposition to the Theological Institution, failed to stop it and seceded. Its Secretary was Robert Eckett, one of the very ablest and most militant of the dissidents. The union of Everett's party with the Association created the 'United Methodist Free Churchs', with an initial membership of 40,000. It is calculated that 100,000 members left the Wesleyan Methodist Church in the course of the crisis, though only a minority of these attached themselves to the new denominations which arose out of it. The whole matter was symptomatic of the stage in the development of social consciousness which the peoples of Europe were now reaching, and its climax was almost simultaneous with that of the Chartist Movement in England and the Year of Revolutions in the rest of Europe. Constitutional reform in Wesleyan Methodism was temporarily delayed by the evil effects of the *Fly Sheets* agitation, but it was bound to come, and Bunting himself opposed it no further. It took the general form of increasing the powers of the Quarterly Meetings of the Circuits, on which laymen sat in large numbers, and giving them the right of direct access to the Conference. Laymen were not finally admitted into the Conference until 1877, although they had been members of all the important Committees of the Conference since 1861. The rights of Wesley's Legal Hundred were, of course, still preserved. Both before and after the admission of laymen to membership of the Conference, the full assembly debated and determined all the matters at issue, and the Legal Hundred met afterwards to ratify the decisions. There is no recorded instance of conflict between the two assemblies.

In 1856 the steady growth of Wesleyan Methodist membership was resumed, and continued until the end of the century. This was in part due to the continuous increases in the industrial and *petit bourgeois* population, but also in part to the success of Methodist evangelism—which included regular 'evangelistic campaigns' in almost every Society—and Methodist pastoral care. It has recently been maintained* that various 'revival' movements in the United States in 1857 and 1858 coalesced, and made a joint impact of great magnitude on Northern Ireland, Wales, and England in 1859 and afterwards. It is claimed that no less than 200,000 members were added to the various Methodist Churches as a result of this. The evidence for the coalescence of the various movements does not seem to be conclusive, and the undoubted increase in the size of the various English denominations at the time is open to more than one interpretation. But it may be that this 'evangelical awakening' was one of the factors leading to the great expansion of Wesleyan Methodist Christianity, though its force is impossible to assess.

There was another factor, in its origin quite outside Methodism. The hubbub in the Church of England caused by the publication of *Tracts for the Times* by Newman and his friends, and the yet greater hubbub caused by the departure of their principal author for the Roman Church, had largely died down. But these events had left an indelible mark on the minds of those English Christians who were incurably Protestant at heart, and there are always many such. Rightly or wrongly they had come to the sorrowful conclusion that 'the Church was in danger', not, as the original Tractarians had supposed, because of the intrusion of the secular power on its prerogatives, but because Newman and his friends were deliberately, though subtly, leading it back to the Papal allegiance. They were not, for the most part, anxious or even willing to leave the Establishment, for an Established Church, whether in England or Scotland or Germany, has a social and intellectual pull which Dissent can never possess; but the Wesleyan Methodist Church, though it exhibited the signs of Dissent, was outspokenly Protestant, and could claim by its size and prominence to be the real representative of the Reformation in England. There is no evidence of numerous 'conversions' from Anglicanism to Methodism, but it is likely that some, at least, who in other circumstances would have become faithful Anglicans became Methodists instead—enough, perhaps, to offset the defection to the Church of England of those Methodists who rose in the social scale and found it more expedient to attend the ministrations of the Parish Church than those of the Chapel.

* By J. E. Orr in *The Second Evangelical Awakening* (1949).

The success of the Oxford Movement had another, and much greater, effect on Wesleyan Methodism. Throughout the first half of the nineteenth century there were many Methodists, notably among the leading ministers, who wished for the breach with the Church of England to be healed, and the suggestion was more than once canvassed that the Methodists should be constituted as a kind of 'Evangelical Order' within the Church of England. In 1834 the Conference gave its explicit blessing to a speech made by Thomas Jackson, then the official editor of Methodist publications, in which he pointed out the strong resemblances between the Church of England and the Wesleyan Methodist Church, and decried those who argued for Disestablishment.

The Methodist temper was very different twenty years later, and the change was very largely due to the attitude and proceedings of the Tractarians. Newman, Keble, and Pusey had found it impossible to make any theological distinction between historic Dissent and new-fangled Methodism; both were equally the product of heresy and schism, and both alike were outside the Catholic Church. If you give a dog a bad name, he will often live up to it, and Methodism responded to the vituperations of the Tracts by becoming a Noncomformist Church more consciously and confidently than ever before. It was greatly helped in this by the apparently Romish practices and beliefs which the Tractarians were seeking to force on their Church. We can see now, from the vantage point of the present, that these men were truly concerned, in their own way, for Christian unity. But at the time all that could be seen was that they were widening and deepening the gulf between Anglicans and Methodists, which could have been bridged, with statesmanship and goodwill, at any time up to 1850, but now became virtually impassable. The literary debate of 1841 between Thomas Jackson, for the Methodists, and E. B. Pusey* shows how wide the separation was to become; and the most serious result of it was that communication between the two communions ceased altogether, and each pursued its own path as if the other did not exist.

Thus Wesleyan Methodism became, what the smaller Methodist Churches had been from their beginnings, a Free

* Pusey charged the Methodists with heresy and antinomianism, and Jackson wrote a pamphlet in reply.

Church, and, as such, it drew much closer than before to the other Free Churches. The champion of this development in Methodism was Hugh Price Hughes. He was a partly Jewish Welshman from Carmarthen who began a series of popular services in St James' Hall, Piccadilly, in 1887. He was by no means a mere revivalist. In fact, the term is better not used of him at all, for, although he was a fiery and passionate preacher, he filled his sermons with theological content, and he was as deeply devoted to the care of men's bodies as he was convinced of the need of their souls for the knowledge of God through Christ. He founded and edited the *Methodist Times*, a weekly which in its prime is said to have been an object of anxious attention to Cabinet Ministers when it next appeared after a debate on social issues. He used this periodical in the first place for the propagation of the idea of Free Church co-operation, and his nonconformity was nothing if not militant. He was primarily responsible for the formation of the National Council of the Free Churches in 1896. This, in Hughes's idea, which finally won the day, was not to be a body representing the Free Churches officially (and therefore, he thought, incapable of free debate from the start), but an assembly of members of local Free Church Councils, and 'a Nonconformist Parliament for our common objects, composed of those who believe in the divinity of our Lord, Jesus Christ'.

Hughes's leadership of his own and other Churches in social matters, often exercised through the *Methodist Times*, was even more effective. Between 1850 and 1900 it seems that the majority of Methodist ministers gradually switched over from an indifference to politics, which occasionally blossomed out into support of Conservative programmes, to an active support for the Liberal cause. The reasons for this change are still obscure; no doubt they have something to do with the awakening of the Christian conscience in general to the evils of industrial exploitation, and still more with the personality and obviously Christian convictions of Mr Gladstone. Hughes embodied and developed the Liberal convictions of his brother ministers—and even preached politics from the pulpit. He was not aiming at the structural alteration of society, however, but at giving every individual the opportunity for a full life by combining evangelism, education, and social services; and at the same time at ridding the national life, especially in London, of its notorious evils. 'Christ came, and the great Revolution began at once,' he said. And the heart of that revolution was a concern for every individual, whatever his character or origin. 'Let us once realize the sacredness of every human being, however poor, however ignorant, however degraded, and tyranny becomes impossible, lust becomes impossible, war becomes impossible.'

Hughes was, in fact, the chief creator of the 'Nonconformist Conscience', which, whatever it has come to mean now, if indeed it still means anything at all, started life as a positive and active concern for human welfare. The name was originally given by a derisive letter in a daily newspaper to the attitude taken up by Hughes in the *Methodist Times* to the continuance of Parnell in his influential position as chairman of the Irish Parliamentary Party after he had been proved guilty of adultery. But Hughes adopted it as a good description of the approach to the affairs of the nation and society at large which he sought to encourage. His last contribution to Church and nation before his untimely death was the development of a chain of 'Central Halls' (following the pattern of the already-established Manchester Mission) in all the great cities of England. These were to be centres of evangelism, fellowship (in the Methodist sense), and social welfare.

Other figures of late nineteenth-century Methodism deserve a brief mention. Most akin to Hughes in ideals was T. B. Stephenson, who in 1870 collected destitute Lambeth children into a house where they could be properly cared for, and so laid the foundations of the now nation-wide and highly organized 'National Children's Home'. The same Dr Stephenson was responsible for the foundation of the Order of Wesley Deaconesses, with a College in Ilkley,* and a mingled vocation to preach, and to exercise pastoral care, and to work among the unprivileged of every kind.

The 'systematic theologian' of the period was William Burt Pope, a man of encyclopaedic mind and an orderly progression of ideas, though not noticeably creative in his thought. But he was no merely academic thinker: when a new Methodist Catechism was being drawn up he persuaded the assembled divines to change the answer to the question '*Who is God?*' From '*An infinite and eternal Spirit*' to '*Our Father*'.

* Now moved to Birmingham.

At the end of the nineteenth century Wesleyan Methodism could claim to be a great and permanent national institution. Already in 1851 (as we know from the census returns of that year) Wesleyan Methodists were one in nine of those who went to church on Sunday morning, and one in four and a half of those who went in the evening. By the end of the century the proportion had largely increased. We have already tried to describe the early Methodists. What sort of people were their late nineteenth-century successors? Novelists, essayists, and Anglican church historians (of an earlier generation) do not, for the most part, give a favourable account of them. They appear as smug, narrow-minded, often hypocritical, opposed to other people's pleasures and incapable of having any of their own except hymn-singing. When Englishmen write about religious people, especially those of the zealous sort, a certain acerbity always creeps in, because of the apparent claim of the religious to criticize the 'ordinary decent Englishman'. When nineteenth-century Methodists are being described, we have to make a further deduction because of the cultural and social differences between the writer and those he is describing (and we have to remember that the Methodists were not sufficiently cultured to describe themselves in any literature which the *litterati* would read). The qualities in Methodists which roused the scorn of the sophisticated were often in reality not moral qualities at all, but lack of culture and *savoir-faire*. Methodists were, in fact, 'vulgar fellows', and it was especially disgusting that they should venture to enter pulpits and preach. They could hardly help being 'vulgar', since they were cut off from the places of higher culture, Oxford and Cambridge, altogether until 1856, and in effect for many years after that.

But when we have made all these allowances, there is no doubt that some of them were self-satisfied with the self-satisfaction of the ignorant, and quite different in their demeanour as worshippers on Sunday and in their attitude as employers of labour on the other days of the week. Yet the great majority of them were always sober, hard-working, kind-hearted citizens, with as much interest in the simpler joys of life as the next man, and often distinguished from him by much greater devotion to the welfare of their families and their place of worship, and to the helping of the underprivileged wherever they were to be found in any part of the world.

If there is one religious fault that can be found with the whole 'body' of Methodists, it is an atomistic doctrine of salvation, and hence an undue preoccupation with the future of their own souls. This was not a special fault of the Methodists. They shared it with all parts of the Christian Church in England; for all had allowed themselves to be infected much too deeply with the prevailing spirit of individualism in economics, politics, social ethics, and religion. Free Churchmen were the worst in this respect, and among them were the Methodists.

When Mr Morgan Phillips, then Secretary of the Labour Party, said that British Socialism was not Marxist but Methodist, he was not thinking, presumably, of the Wesleyan Methodists. It was among the Primitive Methodists, and to a certain extent the other smaller groups, that the first leaders of the British Labour Movement were to be found. The Tolpuddle Martyrs of 1834 were, it is true, Wesleyans. Three of the six founder-members of the abortive Trade Union who were transported to Australia were Wesleyan Methodist Local Preachers, and the meetings of the Union always began with prayer and the renewal of Christian vows. In fact, it was this circumstance that enabled them to be brought for trial—on the evidence of informers planted in the meeting for the purpose—not for forming a Trade Union, which was perfectly legal, but for administering unlawful oaths. But the Wesleyan Methodist Conference disinterested itself completely in their fate, and even took no steps to alleviate the hardships of the convicts' families. By refusing to share the humiliation of the martyrs, it debarred itself from any share in their future glory.

Joseph Rayner Stephens, one of the founders of Chartism, was actually a Wesleyan Methodist minister, but scarcely a typical one. He was a born agitator, and spent much of his ministry denouncing the machinations of the Church of England and the tyranny of Jabez Bunting. He mingled his advocacy of disestablishment with yet more drastic social policies, and introduced his views on all such subjects into his sermons and his conduct of Church life. He was asked to desist from such things, and resigned from the ministry to give his whole time to Chartist agitation. Even among the Chartists he was an extremist, and gave his full support to the use of physical violence when Chartist aims seemed unlikely of fulfilment by purely peaceful means. Wesleyan Methodism can claim neither credit nor discredit for his activities.

It did, however, produce Henry Broadhurst, born in 1840, who organized a stonemasons' union, and obtained an increase of a halfpenny an hour and a decrease of nine hours a week for his workmates. He became a member of the Royal Commission on the condition of the aged poor, and ultimately in 1894 a Member of Parliament. But he also was by no means typical.

But Primitive Methodists were active in the Trades Unions almost from the moment in 1825 at which it became legal for working people to 'combine' for the purpose of redressing their grievances, and they were active, almost, *as* Primitive Methodists. Not, of course, that the Primitive Methodist Conferences associated themselves with Trade Union activities. But it was notorious that Primitive Methodist preachers were taking the lead in these activities up and down the country, and no bar was placed on them. It was natural that Primitive Methodists should act in this way. They themselves were mine-workers, mill-workers, agricultural workers. They knew all about the long hours and filthy conditions for men, women, and children. They were moved to sorrowful anger by what they experienced and observed. Moreover, they knew their Bible, with its constant denunciation of injustice and its uncompromising assertion of love as the only possible basis for human society in the Kingdom of God. And, from long exercise of voice and mind in the services and meetings of their Societies, they were articulate.

So in a large number of places the early Trade Unions were organized as 'chapels' (and the name still lingers), often with small groups under a leader for the payment of subscriptions, in the manner of the Methodist Class Meeting. Meetings often began with extempore prayer, and very often the organizer and the leaders spoke in very much the same way as they did from the pulpit on Sundays, urging a firm reliance on God, a strict control of oneself, and a dauntless opposition to wrong. When the situation seemed to many to call for violence, they favoured peaceful negotiation; when the members were inclined to rest on the results already achieved, they called for ceaseless vigilance.

A long list has been compiled* of Primitive Methodist local preachers who were active in nineteenth-century Trade Unionism. The record of their activities is rarely exciting; it can usually

* By R. F. Wearmouth, in his highly informative books on Methodism and the working classes (see Bibliography).

be put in words like these, which describe the life of one John Bell of County Durham:

> Sixty-seven and a half years a miner, fifty-two years a class leader, forty-six years a local preacher, finally assistant manager of Murton Colliery, chosen as secretary of the Murton Lodge of the Durham Miners' Union, and thereupon dismissed from the colliery.

Two areas of specially intensive Primitive Methodist activity stand out. One is the Durham coalfields, where the unions were founded and fostered until the end of the century by Primitive Methodism. One of its 'activists' was Peter Lee, whose name has been given to one of the new towns in County Durham. He began to work in a cotton mill in Lancashire at the age of nine, and became a 'pit boy' in Durham a year later. By the age of seventeen he was hewing at the coal face. A little later he emigrated, first to America, then to South Africa; and then came back home. He was promoted to checkweighman, appointed to the Executive of the Miners' Association, and elected to the County Council (of which he became Chairman). Throughout his public career he was preaching in Primitive Methodist chapels Sunday by Sunday.

The other main field of operation was agricultural Trade Unionism. The Tolpuddle disaster had sent this into hibernation for many years, but in the seventies it began to emerge. Its principal leader was Joseph Arch. He was brought up in the Church of England, but his adolescent idealism was shocked by the inequalities which it seemed to encourage in its own life. At the age of fourteen he joined the Primitive Methodist Church and the Liberal Party, and remained a faithful member of both for the rest of his life. Preaching on Sundays and addressing political meetings on weekdays seemed to him to be two forms of the same activity. The chief difficulties about the formation and maintenance of a Trade Union among farm workers were their geographical isolation from one another and their slowness to respond to exhortations to better their own lot. Arch's inspiration and persistence overcame both, and he soon had a 'National Trade Union' behind him, demanding bigger wages, an extended franchise, and the nationalization of the land. He was countered by the employers with a large scale lock-out, but the Union survived. During the bad days of the agricultural depression which came soon afterwards, the funds of the Union enabled 700,000 people—surplus workers and their families—to emigrate. In

1884 the rural areas of the country were at last freed from the dominance of Justices of the Peace, and given a certain measure of self-government. As a result, the Union's activities dwindled, since many of its objectives were now attained. But Arch had helped to bring in a new age for the countryside.

Thus the Primitive Methodists—alongside the Christian Socialists, but in a different way—did something to redeem the reputation of the Church in England for indifference, not to say hostility, to the legitimate grievances of the working classes. They exercised an influence wholly disproportionate to the smallness of their numbers and material resources. But they *were* a small body, and they were largely unsupported by their fellow-Christians. It is therefore astonishing to what extent they gave a particular tone to British Trade Unionism and the Labour Movement in general in its early years. Yet it would be purely romantic to suppose that Christianity was more than one powerful ingredient in these movements, or even that anything more than a small minority of working people received the spiritual ministrations of the Christian Church in any form. The Church has not *lost* the allegiance of the British working man; it has never had it—though the Primitive Methodists and the Christian Socialists did their best. By the end of the nineteenth century, there is good reason to suppose that the influence of both these groups had passed its peak, and that the leadership of labour was already moving into other hands.

Not even the smaller Methodist Churches were always able to contain the revolutionary zeal of some of their members. William Booth was first a Wesleyan local preacher, then (no doubt in the interests of freedom) a minister successively of the Wesleyan Reform Committee and the Methodist New Connexion. He found it impossible to reconcile his passion for ministering to the poor, especially in the lowest parts of London, with the requirements of the congregations to which he had been appointed, and resigned from the ministry in 1861. With his wife Catherine, certainly as strong and able a personality as himself, he founded the Christian Revival Association, which became in 1872 the Salvation Army. He was convinced that only a strict military organization (still preserved today) would meet the needs of those whom he had in mind, and installed himself as General. The achievements both spiritual and material of the Salvation Army, in those sections of our civilization which the respectable communions of Christendom had forborne to enter, are well-known. William and Catherine did their work in spite of dispensing with the Sacraments of the Church and an ordained ministry. William's *In Darkest England and the Way Out* (1890) remains as a lurid testimony to the state of affairs with which the Army has struggled manfully to deal; and some of the social measures which it suggests, such as farm colonies and rescue homes, are still being tried out today.

The nineteenth century was a period in which the ideas, organization, and methods bequeathed by John Wesley to the Methodists were developed and deployed over a large area of British life—not without some modification and corruption, but with considerable success. The heart of the Methodist Movement remained at first in the Sacrament, the Class Meeting, and the Preaching Service. But opposition to the Oxford Movement and assimilation to historic nonconformity tended, as the century wore on, to take the emphasis away from the Sacraments—and gradually to some extent from the Class Meeting, which was becoming formalized and a little artificial—to the Preaching Service. For Wesley, the Preaching Service was an addendum to the regular liturgical services of the Church of England. A fair number of Wesleyan Methodist Churches still retained the practice of Matins every Sunday morning. But in the great majority of them, and in all the chapels of the smaller Methodist Churches, the Preaching Service came to stand alone, as *the* service of public worship. This is reflected in Methodist Church architecture of the period: in the well-proportioned but somewhat heavy 'Brunswick' chapels of the first half of the century; in the neo-Gothic but sometimes not entirely ungraceful structures of the second half; in the barn-like, box-like erections (designed solely, so far as one can see, to allow the greatest possible number of people to see the preacher) of the 'disruption' chapels in the industrial areas; in the simple, often crude, meeting-houses of all types of village Methodists. The pulpit (which is often a vast rostrum) stands in the central place, often with the choir seats behind, always with the holy table below. But in those days (and until the First World War) preaching, even mediocre preaching, could hold large congregations together. So anti-liturgicalism seemed to be justified; and due place was certainly given to the Word of God.

CHAPTER EIGHT

A World Church

In one of the principal offices in New York of the Methodist Church of America there is—or was—a map indicating the whereabouts of Methodist activity throughout the world. On it there is no indication of any Methodism in Great Britain at all. This fact, though somewhat galling to the English Methodists who have observed it, does at least indicate the immense preponderance in size of American Methodism over its British counterpart. But Methodism in America sprang directly from the preaching and organizing activities of John Wesley. He had some personal knowledge of life in the American colonies, though it may have given him no pleasure to recall it, and he never lost his interest in their needs. When the time came, he was happy to pass on to others the task in which he himself had signally failed.

The ground had to some extent been prepared by the restless activities of George Whitefield, as he hurried hither and thither to preach and raise money for his orphanage in Georgia. But the first real Methodist Societies in America were founded by immigrants from Ireland, where they had been converted by John Wesley. One was in Sam's Creek, not far from Baltimore in Maryland, and the man responsible was Robert Strawbridge from Ulster. He was, officially, a local preacher, but in fact he carried on a wide itinerant ministry in an area where the ordinary rules of Methodism could hardly be expected to apply. When Strawbridge was eventually integrated into a regularly constituted Methodist Connexion, he found the regulations extremely hampering.

The other was in New York. Philip Embury and his wife came from County Limerick, but their origins were in the Palatinate. The armies of Louis XIV drove thousands of Germans from there to find refuge in England, then Ireland, then America. Embury was a local preacher in Ireland, but he joined the Lutheran Church in New York, and gave up preaching. But his cousin,

Mrs Barbara Heck, was of sterner stuff, and thought that Methodism was as necessary in America as in Ireland. So she roused him from his inactivity, and soon there was a Society in New York. It was reinforced shortly afterwards by the arrival of Thomas Webb, captain in the British Army, another convert of John Wesley and an extremely forceful personality.

Both of these Societies were under way by 1768, and in the following year Wesley's Conference sent two volunteers, Richard Boardman and Joseph Pilmoor, to take over and develop the work. From then until the War of Independence there was a steady growth of Methodist Societies, most of all in Virginia. The main impetus was given by the arrival from England in 1771 of Francis Asbury, at the age of twenty-six. Asbury was a blacksmith from West Bromich who became a travelling preacher. 'Our brethren in America call aloud for help,' said Wesley to his Bristol Conference; and Asbury immediately volunteered. A month later his ship slipped out of the little port of Pill, near Bristol, and he was never seen again in England. His relentless determination and his unquenchable spirit of adventure soon gave him a commanding position in American Methodism, and he moulded its destinies for the next fifty years. He discovered soon after his arrival that the preachers were tending to concentrate their efforts on the towns that had a settled population. He saw quite clearly that to restrict the Methodist enterprise to these would remove it from the growing-points of American life, and he begged his seniors to keep the preachers travelling on the ever-extending frontiers. In the end he persuaded them to adopt a rule by which no preacher stayed anywhere for longer than six months—with the result that where the men of enterprise and initiative went, there went also the Methodist preacher as one of them, and the Methodist 'circuit-rider' became one of the formative influences of American civilization. Asbury himself is said to have travelled more than a quarter of a million miles. At the unveiling of an equestrian statue in Washington of the 'prophet of the long road', as the American Methodists call him, the reigning President of the United States saluted him as 'one of the builders of our nation', and this was no mere American flowery compliment.

Just as Asbury was getting into his stride, John Wesley, of all people, dealt the Methodist preachers a damaging blow. In 1768 he had written: 'I do not defend the measures which have been taken in regard to America; I doubt whether any man can defend them on the foot of law, equity, or prudence.' But in 1775 he came out with a *Calm Address to the American Colonists* (in fact an abridgement of Samuel Johnson's *Texation no Tyranny*) in which he sternly condemned the aspirations and methods of the disgruntled Americans. The English Government began to shower unwonted—and unwanted—favours on the leader of the Methodists, and his enemies took the opportunity of rubbing in their view of him as a deceiver; Augustus Toplady in *An Old Fox Tarr'd and Feather'd* jeered at him for purloining a 'bundle of Lilliputian shafts out of Dr Johnson's pincushion'. Wesley was not in the least disconcerted, and published other pamphlets to the same effect as the *Calm Address*. But the news of his attitude crossed the Atlantic, and created the strong impression that the Methodists were all diehard Tories. They were persecuted in various ways, and their influence ceased to grow. When the War of Independence came, the Methodist preachers who were native Americans took the side of their fellow-countrymen, and gradually regained their confidence. The preachers from England found their position intolerable, and one by one they all departed, except Asbury. He went on with his work, and maintained a strict neutrality. When the war was over, he seems to have found little difficulty in persuading the victorious Americans that he was their faithful friend, and his English origin was rarely if ever held against him.

We have already seen how Wesley handled the crisis caused by the lack of ordained ministers in the new America. When Thomas Coke, appointed as Superintendent by Wesley, arrived in New York at the end of 1784 accompanied by Whatcoat and Vasey, who had been ordained as presbyters by Wesley, the time had come to settle the constitution of American Methodism. The notable thing about the way it was settled is that Wesley's wishes were by no means in all cases observed. The first Conference was held in Baltimore, consisting of sixty out of the eighty-one preachers then in the active ministry. Wesley's *Sunday Service of the Methodists*, an adaptation of the Book of Common Prayer for American use, was adopted (though it was gradually superseded in practice by less formal modes of worship); so also were Wesley's *Twenty-Four Articles of Religion*, which were those of the Thirty-Nine which Wesley thought most important (the American Conference added one, *Of the Rulers of the United*

States of America). The *Form of Discipline* which was made the basis of all administrative measures was based on Wesley's own procedure in England, and it included the circuit system and the itinerancy.

But other decisions of the Conference were not equally to Wesley's taste. He had instructed Coke to ordain Asbury, and had nominated him as Superintendent. But Asbury asserted that he was not to be Superintendent on Wesley's nomination, and insisted on unanimous election by the Conference before either Coke or he exercised this office. The title given to the Church was the 'Methodist Episcopal Church'—which was *not* chosen by Wesley. A College, to be called Cokesbury College, for the sons of preachers, was opened, and provoked a letter from John Wesley to Asbury:

> Both the Doctor and you differ from me. I study to be little: you study to be great. I creep, you strut along. I found a school: you a College! Nay, and call it after your own names! O beware, do not seek to be something!

Eight years later the college was burned down, and the conflagration persuaded Asbury that God did not intend the Methodist Episcopal Church to embark on educational schemes.

Worst of all, Asbury and Coke allowed themselves to be called Bishops—as a natural consequence from the title of the Church.

> How can you, how dare you suffer yourself to be called Bishop? I shudder, I start, at the very thought! Men may call me a knave or a fool, a rascal, a scoundrel, and I am content; but they shall never by my consent call me Bishop! For my sake, for God's sake, for Christ's sake put a full end to this!

—wrote Wesley. But to no effect. The new title remains to this day. The incident goes to show that the American Methodists, much though they honoured the 'venerable founder' of the Methodist Societies, were not going to be ordered about by him. In 1784 the Methodist Episcopal Church of America became, in fact, completely separate from its parent body.

Wesley's aspersions on the arrogance of Asbury and Coke were largely derived from his close knowledge of the character of the latter. Coke was an irrepressibly eager, zealous, and enterprising little Welshman. But he was also ambitious and impetuous. When he arrived in America, he no doubt thought that he had been called to play a Wesley's part among the callow and illiterate

Americans. Such a part was reserved for Asbury, and in any case Coke had greatly exaggerated in his own mind the callowness and illiteracy of the ex-colonists. So he met with many disappointments and caused much ill-feeling as he tried to exercise the rights which he did not possess. Perhaps the worst example of his tactlessness was when in 1791, entirely without authority from anyone, he proposed a scheme of union with the Protestant Episcopal Church, on the basis of the re-ordination of the Methodist preachers and the appointment of Asbury and himself as Bishops in the united Church. But the rebuffs which he received and the indiscretions which he committed did not daunt him or sour his spirit, and, as we shall see, his eventual retirement from the American scene gave him new opportunities for exercising his considerable gifts.

For the fifty years from 1790 to 1840 the Methodist Episcopal Church increased with astonishing rapidity, powerfully led by the circuit-riders, who took the Methodist Gospel across the Alleghanies to the furthest reaches of the American advance. Their methods were crude, their message was stripped to the barest essentials, and their hymns included such ditties as the following (entitled 'Shout Old Satan's Kingdom Down'):

> This day my soul has caught on fire, Hallelujah!
> I feel that Heaven is coming nigher, O glory Hallelujah!
>
> *Chorus:*
> Shout, shout, we're gaining ground, Hallelujah!
> We'll shout old Satan's kingdom down, Hallelujah!
>
> When Christians pray, the Devil runs,
> And leaves the field to Zion's sons—
> (*Hallelujahs and chorus as before*)
>
> One single saint can put to flight
> Ten thousand blustering sons of night—
> (*Hallelujahs and chorus as before*)

But they succeeded. Asbury's objections to educational schemes were gradually overcome, and colleges and schools sprang up everywhere in the wake of the circuit-riders. By 1819 the Church was sufficiently sure of its place in America and its ability to go on extending its work to be ready to contemplate missionary work among non-Americans. The first activities of the Missionary Society were among the Wyandot Indians, living in a reservation in Central Ohio. The work was soon extended to include Indians living on both sides of the Rocky Mountains.

But the slavery controversy checked the advance and divided the Church. The original *Form of Discipline* included a plan to 'extirpate the abomination of slavery', and ordered every member to free his slaves within a certain length of time, though it made exceptions where state laws prevented emancipation. In the Southern States the exceptions proved to be much stronger than the rule, and as the economy of the South came to be more and more dependent on cotton, for which slaves were deemed to be a necessity, the Methodists there acquiesced in the continuance of the institution of slavery, though opposed to it in principle. Meanwhile in the North the movement against slavery became more and more powerful, and attracted the warm allegiance of the majority of Methodists, leaders and members alike. The matter came to be hotly debated in Conference, despite all efforts to have it ruled out of order, but until 1844 the supporters of slavery could count on a majority which would prevent any drastic action. In that year the balance shifted, and the situation of a certain Bishop Andrew, a mild and modest man who had become a slaveowner by bequest and marriage, was made the *casus belli*. He offered to resign his bishopric, but the Southern bishops would not hear of it, fought to the last ditch a resolution to depose him, and lost.

This brought matters to a crisis. The Southern bishops were first of all allowed by a vote of the Conference to secede and form a separate Church, and took advantage of this permission. Then the Conference changed its mind and repudiated the Plan of Separation, thus turning the seceders into traitors to their Church. There was a long period of bitterness, and of lawsuits about property, and when the Civil War broke out in 1861 the Methodist Episcopal Church and the Methodist Episcopal Church, South, were ranged against each other in their approaches to the throne of grace for victory. After the war the bitterness gradually subsided, though the treatment of the vanquished by the victors inflicted many scars which have even now not completely healed. The slavery issue resulted also in the formation of three powerful Negro Methodist Churches* in the South, and they remain independent to this day.

* The African Methodist Episcopal Church; the African Methodist Episcopal Church Zion; and the Coloured (now 'Christian') Methodist Episcopal Church.

The difficult years of reconstruction were followed in the last twenty years of the nineteenth century by a wave of affluence, and both the white Methodist Episcopal Churches shared in it. They had continued to grow rapidly, and now a large proportion of their members were in very comfortable circumstances. In other words, as in England, the Methodists were thrifty and hard-working, and when the boom came they all gained heavily from it; perhaps for this reason they never won the support of the more indigent members of the population, most of whom were immigrants from the poorer parts of Europe, bringing their form of Christianity with them. Hence came about the conditions which are very clearly observable in American Church life today: the class and wealth structure of the country is closely reflected in denominational membership.

With success and wealth went a certain loosening of doctrinal and disciplinary rigidity. Gradually there came over the theological scene in Methodism—as indeed in all the middle-class Churches of the country—a haze of liberalism, not unmixed with sentimentality, and precision of dogmatic statement came to be regarded as something of a breach of taste. At the same time the Class Meeting slipped into obscurity, and the purely social activities of each congregation increased. The general effect in the twentieth century has been to obscure denominational boundaries, and make American Protestantism a unity in very slight diversity.

But there were mitigating features of great importance. The first was in the field of education. It has to be remembered that in the United States the government is religiously neutral, and that no form of Christianity may be taught in the State (properly called 'public') schools. The Churches, therefore, and not least the Methodist Churches, have taken in hand their own religious education, by means of a far more elaborate system of youth work and Sunday Schools than has ever been attempted in Britain. American Methodism has spent vast resources in building up colleges and universities—some of high status, others catering for what in England would be regarded as sixth-form studies—in every State of the Union, to provide Christian higher education, not only for theological students but for those studying every conceivable subject. More than a third of the universities and colleges now operating in the United States are of Methodist foundation.

The second was in the field of overseas missions. And this field was a vast one. North India, Mexico, most of the other States of Latin America, Japan, Cuba, Korea, Formosa, and many parts of Africa—all these and many more were included in the American Methodist programme before the end of the century. The outstanding figure in this development was William Taylor. He preached first in California, not then included among the United States, and in 1862 went on to Australia, Tasmania, southern Africa, Ceylon, India, and Chile. Wherever he could he made the missions self-supporting, by founding a school which charged fees and so sustained the missionaries. This was more successful in some places than others, but where it was economically impracticable Taylor introduced and organized local industries.

Thirdly, there was the field of social service. When British Methodists take it into their heads to criticize their American cousins, they usually point out that American Methodism is activistic and extroverted, with too little attention to theological issues and the devotional life. There is substance in this charge; yet it does not entitle us to forget the immense works of charity for which American Methodists have always been responsible in every area of human need. This concern for the needs of others took the particular form, in the years just before and after the First World War, of what is called the 'social Gospel'. This means the interpretation of the New Testament as being primarily concerned with the setting up of the Kingdom of God (thought of as an international and social Utopia) on earth. It is associated in particular with the name of William Rauschenbusch, a Baptist, but churchmen of every denomination in America were active in promulgating it, and many Methodists were to the fore. Disillusionment in the years of the slump killed this version of the Gospel—deservedly, for it omits the whole eschatological dimension of Scripture, is too optimistic about human nature, and makes the Kingdom more human than divine. But it served a good end while it lasted in kindling the sympathy of many Americans for their less fortunate neighbours in other parts of the world, and showing them that the Gospel is not a purely personal affair.

The general assimilation of all American Protestant Churches, and the dying away of old enmities, made possible the peaceful reunion of the two Methodist Episcopal Churches into the Methodist Church of America in 1939, with a membership of something like nine millions, and a 'community membership' of three times the size. It disputes with the Baptist Churches the honour of being the largest Protestant denomination in the United States. It became larger still in 1968 with the accession of the Evangelical United Brethren Church, and was re-named the United Methodist Church.

The whole of this development, from 1784 until very recent times, has taken place in complete isolation from British Methodism; yet many of the features of historic Methodism are common to both its main modern types—chiefly, an evangelistic mission to all the world, a disciplined organization, an emphasis on fellowship in the Spirit, and a zeal for social holiness.

The world-wide evangelistic mission was very prominent in nineteenth-century British Methodism. It was, of course, implicit in John Wesley's whole conception of the Gospel, and found rather naïve expression in Thomas Coke's *Plan of the Society for the Establishment of Missions amongst the Heathen* (1784) and *Address to the Pious and Benevolent*, which was published in 1786, a little while before the better-known appeal of William Carey to the Northamptonshire Baptist Association to found a missionary society. Coke pointed out the heathen condition of the peoples of India and Africa, and also of rural Ireland, Wales, and north-western Scotland, and appealed for volunteers and subscriptions from all and sundry. John Wesley rebuked Coke for impractical idealism, and concentrated on his plans for America. But Coke was not to be denied. In 1786 he was on his way to America with three preachers for that country, and his ship was so buffeted and damaged by Atlantic storms (which frightened the crew into throwing the preachers' sermons, and almost their persons, Jonah-like, into the sea) that they were forced to take refuge in Antigua. Coke and his companions disembarked, and were walking up the main street of St John's, when they met a man with a lantern, to whom Coke introduced himself, and then recognized him as a shipwright from Chatham called John Baxter, who was continuing the Methodist services started by Nathaniel Gilbert, Speaker of the House of Assembly of Antigua. The same evening Coke preached to a thousand negroes. His appetite whetted by this first real experience of 'missionary' work, Coke left his three companions to continue it, and went back to England to plead the cause of the West Indian mission to the British Conference.

The Conference agreed to recognize Coke as its 'Agent' in the West Indies, and later as the General Superintendent of Foreign Missions. His methods were boldly conceived and wide-ranging, but a trifle improvident and not without hints of personal ambition. The Conference was compelled to keep him on a fairly tight rein, and to provide him with a 'Committee of Finance and Advice' for the purposes of reasonable control. In 1813, by a passionate speech to the Conference in Liverpool, he obtained permission for seven missionaries, including himself (at the age of sixty-six), to go to Ceylon, one to Java, and one to the Cape of Good Hope. He himself died on the voyage. In the same year the Wesleyan Methodist Missionary Society was set up, with the strong support of Jabez Bunting, and Coke had won his point.

For many years the West Indies held first place in the affections of missionary enthusiasts in British Methodism. From the first the missionaries there were opposed to slavery, and roused the bitter resentment of the Dutch and British traders, who thrashed their negroes for attending Methodist services. Emancipation in 1834 brought the negroes in their thousands to the Methodist and Baptist Churches for services of thanksgiving, for that was where their friends and champions worshipped. In the varying and difficult economic conditions which resulted from emancipation, the missionaries suffered many changes of fortune. There were many revivals and many subsequent disappointments. Prominent among the latter were the frequent discoveries that apparent conversion to Christianity had no effect on financial or sexual morals. Yet, because education went on alongside evangelism, a solid Christian community was built up. At one time it seemed so strong that it was decided to make the Methodist Church of the West Indies independent of the Mother Church. But this proved to be economically and personally unwise, and independence was withdrawn. Yet it was a foretaste of developments in the second half of the present century.

Once the Missionary Society was properly launched, the fields of activity multiplied with great speed. They are too numerous to be described in detail. Sierra Leone and Canada were high on the list in point of time; and a small start in Namaqualand, north-west of Cape Town, was made in 1816. It was characteristic of the way Methodist missions spread that the first missionaries in this last area, Barnabas Shaw and his wife, were sent out in answer to an appeal from Methodists in the British garrison. They preached to the Africans only, but as the work developed the settlers also were drawn into the Church. By 1881 Methodism was so strongly established in South Africa that a separate South African Conference was set up. The Church there today has the largest non-European membership of any, and is second only to the Dutch Reformed Church in total size. The problems of race and *apartheid* have engaged it more acutely than any other Church, because of its peculiar sympathy with African aspirations and its knowledge of African weakness and strength.

Further north, the virtual founder of the mission to the Gold Coast (now Ghana) was Thomas Birch Freeman, son of a negro and a white woman, who arrived in 1838. He travelled on so wide a scale that the Missionary Society was unable to cope with all the stations which he set up; and he included the building of schools and model farms within his scope.

In the Ivory Coast, or French West Africa, there were virtually no Protestants until a strange figure appeared at the beginning of the present century, carrying a Bible and a wooden cross at the top of a bamboo staff, and calling on the people to forsake and burn their idols and fetishes, and turn to the Cross of Jesus. This was 'Prophet' Harris, a Grebo from the black Republic of Liberia; he was a Christian all his life, but a lukewarm one until he was sixty. In his younger days he had given much trouble to the authorities by his nationalistic agitation, but during his third imprisonment he was instructed by the Angel Gabriel to take the Gospel to those who had never heard of Christ. On his release, he obeyed the instruction with great enthusiasm, and with so much success that the French imprisoned him again and deported him. Before he left his people he told them to wait for the coming of the missionaries, who would instruct them more fully in the faith. They waited patiently for ten years. In 1924 their existence and the work of Harris were brought to light by a Methodist missionary, who reported them to his Society in London; and since then the Methodist missionaries have been at work in the area.

Western Nigeria, like the Gold Coast, owed much to Freeman, and it was here that the missionaries of the Primitive Methodists concentrated their main effort. But they also went to Northern Rhodesia, where the Wesleyan Methodists had already arrived. There was ample room for both, especially when the discovery of copper near the frontier of the Belgian Congo brought hundreds of thousands of Africans to the mines. The United Methodist Free Churches were represented in Sierra Leone—not least in Mendeland.

In all these areas doctors, nurses, and teachers followed hard in the wake of the missionaries; and the contribution of Methodism was only a part of the immense missionary enterprise in Africa of all the Churches in Christendom during the nineteenth century. It is not surprising that at the outbreak of the First World War ninety-five per cent of all education south of the Sahara was in the hands of the Missionary Societies.

In Asia the progress was necessarily much slower. For the religions which there confronted the Christian missionary were as developed in their ideas as the one that was being imported, and had the additional advantage of symbolizing the proud nationalism of the ancient peoples of the East. In Ceylon there were very few converts for nearly a century after Coke's dramatic summons to the Methodists to evangelize it. In India the missionaries were limited to Mysore and Madras, even so late as Queen Victoria's Jubilee. The early attempts to reach the high-caste people had failed utterly, and it became a matter of policy to pursue evangelism by the indirect path of schools, colleges, and hospitals. But the Indians, though very willing to make use of the facilities thus offered, felt no obligation to transfer their allegiance to the religion of their benefactors. No one can assess, of course, the effect of Christian ethical teaching on the thinking of enlightened Hindus, such as the great Mahatma Gandhi, but the plain fact is that the number of professed Christians among them remained depressingly low throughout the century. Missionaries of all denominations told the same story. Then suddenly, beginning about 1880 and continuing into the twentieth century, mass movements to Christianity of the outcastes swept over large areas of South India, most of all in Hyderabad; there were many outbursts of persecution, but the whole missionary scene was changed.

It was granted to South India, perhaps because of the particular way the Church there grew, to be the home of the first concrete expression of the modern spirit of Christian unity. At least since 1910, when the non-Roman missionary societies met at Edinburgh to harmonize their policy, overlapping between the missionary societies operating in the area had been largely avoided; each denomination had its own districts to work. The Congregational and Presbyterian Churches in South India had been united in 1908. In 1919, under strong pressure from Christian Indians, who could see no reason why the divisions of British Christianity should be perpetuated on Indian soil to the lasting damage of Christian witness to Hindus and Muslims, the Anglicans began to discuss organic union with the united Presbyterians and Congregationalists. The Methodists joined the conversations in 1925, and the final scheme for the new Church of South India was agreed to by the Churches in South India in 1942 and consummated in 1947. It was laid down that the ministries of all the uniting Churches, episcopal and non-episcopal, should be recognized, but that no congregation should be compelled to have a minister whose orders they did not acknowledge. The constitution of the new Church is episcopal, though the bishop's powers are limited by the presence of a Synod. All ordinations from the beginning of the Church have been episcopal. The Methodist Church in India joined enthusiastically in the project, and the majority of Methodists in Britain strongly approved it.

The needs of the times and the example of South India have produced union schemes, on slightly different lines, for North India and Ceylon. The Church of North India came into existence in 1970.

In China, the history of Methodist missions is even more chequered. Changes of attitude on the part of the Chinese Government in the nineteenth century, from hatred of all things European to a passionate love, and then back again to bitter hatred, gave all the societies a precarious position in the country. Perhaps the non-denominational China Inland Mission battled most successfully with the changing situation. But there were Wesleyan Methodist missionaries at various points; and in south-west China, Bible Christians had been working with only small success until suddenly in 1904 the Miaos, a subject people of great antiquity, burst into their mission at Chaotung and demanded to hear the Gospel. So began a mass movement directed by Samuel Pollard, who had to invent a script and a grammar, and then translate the Bible into the Miao language, for his simple converts. Chinese Christians here and elsewhere have since then been through many vicissitudes, and the end of hardship is certainly not yet. But when the Communists drove out the last

Christian missionaries in 1951, there was a native Church throughout China that was able to stand on its own feet. News since then has been painfully scanty.

In Australia today the Methodist Church, by reason of its vigorous evangelism and educational institutions, is probably the most powerful of all the non-Roman Churches, but it started in a very small way, probably in Sydney in 1815. From Australia it spread not only to Tasmania but to New Zealand, where it soon gained a footing, not least among the apparently untameable Maoris. Australian missionaries went to the Friendly Islands, and converted first of all King Tubou of Tonga, and then King Taufa-ahau of Haabai; or rather, Taufa-ahau first of all heard the story of Christ from a shipwrecked sailor who expected to be eaten by the natives, but was requested by the king to play the part of an amateur missionary instead; the real missionaries arrived later and completed the conversion. Taufa-ahau changed his name to George, became paramount King of Tonga, and completely transformed the social and legal system of the Tongese. His granddaughter, Queen Salote of Tonga, a picturesque figure at the Coronation of Queen Elizabeth II, was a Methodist class leader, and Queen Elizabeth worshipped with her in a Methodist Church when she paid a State visit to the Friendly Islands.

British Methodists were reluctant to extend their Church into the Protestant parts of Europe, thinking perhaps that Luther and Calvin had reformed the Churches there in suitable fashion. But the American Methodists had no such inhibitions, and there are minority Methodist Churches in Switzerland, the Scandinavian countries, and Germany, as well as in Belgium, Austria, and Poland. The German Methodist Church is the most vigorous of these. It resulted from the return of Germans to their homeland, some from England and some from America, after becoming Methodists on their travels. Those who came from England began Methodist Societies in Württemberg, those from America in Hamburg and the surrounding country. The Societies were eventually united into one Church with an American polity, and indeed all these European Methodist Churches are ultimately linked with the Methodist Church of the United States. There is a Methodist Church of British origin in Italy, where it has much in common with the ancient Waldensian Church; and there were small ones in France and Spain before they were united with other Protestant Churches*; there is one in Portugal.

It is fashionable to deride the nineteenth-century missionary: to say that he foisted Western civilization, and trousers, on the innocent natives; that he terrified them into the kingdom of God by holding them over the brink of Hell; that he disrupted tribal life without providing anything better; that he simply prepared the way for the commercial exploiter; that his converts, especially in the mass movement areas, were only 'rice Christians'. There is, of course, some force in all these criticisms (except for the one about the brink of Hell); but many of them spring from men's natural desire to excuse themselves for not doing what they ought to have done by criticizing the only people who have attempted to do it, and possibly in some cases from the unconscious desire to keep subject peoples in their place. The positive achievements of the missionaries have a secure place in history. They banished degrading superstitions and customs from the lives of millions, and helped them to feel secure in the love of a Father who intended nothing but their good in this life and the life to come; they taught them to develop their powers of mind and memory and imagination and self-expression, and introduced them to the full life which had been denied them; they showed them the benefits of hygiene and sanitation, cured innumerable sufferers, and conquered many crippling diseases; they built up Churches which are now an example and an inspiration to the rest of Christendom; and they paved the way for the self-realization and self-determination of African and Asian peoples which is the most striking and most permanent feature of the present century. Europeans and Americans may sometimes be daunted by the rise of new nations and the effect on the world that they are already producing. Most of the leaders of the new nations, at least in Africa, were trained in missionary schools, and some say that everything that they know they owe to the missionaries. The rise was bound to come in any case. How much more terrifying it would be if it were led by those whose only knowledge of the white man was derived from the representatives of commercial and imperial interests!

*** In France there is still a small Methodist Church.**

CHAPTER NINE

Modern Methodism

There is evidence for the view that the start of the present century marked the climax of the success and influence of the Churches in Great Britain, and perhaps in particular of the Free Churches. We have seen why Wesleyan Methodism, at least, was prosperous and self-confident. Its churches were full, and large ones were being built in many parts of the country; there was a steady stream of men who felt themselves called into its ministry, and it was possible to select only the best; the Central Halls were coping with the social needs of the great cities; conversions were taking place all over the Connexion, mostly, no doubt, among those who were brought up in the Methodist fold, but also among the people gathered in by evangelistic campaigns. The nation at large was aware of the existence of a well-organized 'pressure group' for the attainment of certain social objectives and for the carrying out of a certain educational policy, and the 'Nonconformist Conscience', with Methodists as its chief exponents, was a force which no politician dared to neglect. The 'cultured despisers' of evangelical religion could poke fun at the narrowness of Methodist piety and the rigidity of Methodist morals, but they could not deny the spiritual earnestness and the effective concern for the welfare of the whole of mankind which marked out the sons and daughters of John Wesley.

The many-sidedness of modern Methodism was embodied in the character and career of John Scott Lidgett (1854–1953),* who stepped into the place of leadership left vacant by the death of Hugh Price Hughes. He was prevented from going to one of the older universities by the early death of his father, but made his way from a firm of insurance and shipping brokers to University College, London, and from there into the Wesleyan Methodist Ministry. After a number of ordinary circuit appointments, he

* He was rather curiously omitted from the otherwise excellent *Dictionary of the Christian Church* (ed. by F. L. Cross, 1957).

went to Bermondsey, by the permission of the Conference, to found a Settlement on the lines laid down by Arnold Toynbee and Samuel Barnett. He stayed in Bermondsey almost throughout the rest of his very long life, but his work branched out of it in many directions. He wrote several major works of theology, of which the most notable was *The Fatherhood of God* (1902), in which he develops the thought of his mentor, Frederick Denison Maurice, and shows that the conception of God's Fatherhood embraces all the divine attributes. He took a leading part in all the 'politics' of Methodism, especially in the manifold discussions which preceded Methodist Union in 1932, and was deservedly elected President of the Uniting Conference in that year. He was the constant representative of Wesleyan Methodism, and of the Free Churches, in the conversations which marked the early years of the Ecumenical Movement, and especially in those which followed the Lambeth Appeal of 1920; he looked upon the rapprochement of the Free Churches, which he did much to foster, and their reunion, which he hoped for, as vital steps towards the reunion of all Christendom, and not as an alliance to meet the common foe which lesser men in the Free Churches were apt to consider the object of the whole operation.

For eleven years he was Editor of the *Methodist Times*, which Hugh Price Hughes had founded, but he probably exercised a greater public influence by sitting first on the London School Board, and then on the London County Council, as Councillor and as Alderman, Deputy Chairman of the Education Committee, and Leader of the Progressive Party. He also found time to be Vice-Chancellor of the University of London for two years.

He was, in fact, the William Temple of Methodism, and, according to many, the greatest Methodist since Wesley. His greatness in the world of ideas is shown by the fact that he wrote and said fifty years ago, especially in the field of ecumenical theology, many of the things that modern theologians are painfully working out today. In the world of practical affairs, his greatest influence was in the fields of education and what used to be called social welfare. So Methodism's part in these matters, inspired by his example, and culminating in its contributions to life today deserves to be chronicled at this point.

John Wesley taught his people from the start to be vitally interested in education. 'Preach expressly on education at least once in the year, when you preach on Kingswood,' he wrote to one of his preachers. '"But," you say, "I have no gift for it." Gift or no gift, you must preach! Else you are not called to be a Methodist preacher.'

His own foundation at Kingswood went through many vicissitudes during his lifetime and throughout the nineteenth century. It came to be limited to the sons of Methodist ministers, and it was the duty of Methodist Societies to make annual subscriptions for its maintenance, for the right to have his sons at Kingswood without fees was part of the minister's stipend, and his way of compensating for the educational disadvantages of perpetual itinerancy. It was transferred to its present magnificent site on Lansdown, above the city of Bath, in 1852, and there began its progress from a denominational institution to a national public school. Its great nineteenth-century headmaster was Thomas George Osborn (1866–85), and the opening of Oxford and Cambridge to non-Anglicans gave chances of advancement to Kingswood boys which they were not slow to take. In the present century the outstanding headmaster has been Alfred Barrett Sackett, who retired from the post, after holding it for thirty-one years, in 1959. Before he began his work, the school had been opened to the sons of laymen of all denominations, and this had helped to broaden its outlook. Sackett transformed the discipline and the curriculum till the school was as hospitable to the sciences as to the classics, to the arts as to the sciences, to out-of-school activities as to examination subjects, and to handicraft as to sport, and could hold its head high with the greatest public schools in the land in all these activities. The school has never wavered from Wesley's ideal of a 'Christian family', and Sackett made it plain that he regarded all the subjects on the time-table as explorations of God's universe and took immense pains to focus them all in the carefully-ordered services of the School Chapel. Kingswood is Methodism's principal contribution to the emerging conception of Christian Education as it is understood today.

It is well known that popular education in this country really began with the Sunday Schools set up by evangelical Christians towards the end of the eighteenth century. They taught the three Rs as a necessary preparation for the study of the Bible. Wesley, of course, encouraged the growth of such schools in his Societies, and the Wesleyan Methodist Conference organized them so successfully that in 1834 more than a third of a million children and 60,000 teachers were in Wesleyan Methodist Sunday Schools. The mutually competing groups of 'voluntary' day schools, started for the Anglicans in 1811 by Andrew Bell, and for the Nonconformists in 1814 by Joseph Lancaster, did not at first arouse Methodism to enter the same field. But in 1843, when the State was still painfully hesitating as to the part it could play in a sphere already bedevilled by Anglican-Nonconformist conflict, the Conference decided to take a hand in the affair. During the next forty years it built 850 schools.

The moving spirit in this development was John Scott. He was in no sense actuated by sectarian motives; he was simply anxious that Methodism should help to do the task which was being so shamefully neglected by the State and so seriously impeded by denominational rivalries. That his aims were broad and enlightened is shown by the wholehearted approval which he gained from Matthew Arnold, who tended to dismiss all Nonconformists as ungainly Philistines. Scott was largely responsible for the opening in 1851 of Westminster College for the training of men and women teachers. (Another college, for women, Southlands in Wimbledon, was opened in 1872.) He was himself the first Principal, and it was in this capacity that he came to know Arnold, who inspected the college from time to time. Scott told his students:

> It is mind that you have to draw out, and mould, and fit for its duties to itself, to mankind and to its Maker. From the child's first entrance into your school, your object is to train him to think, and to teach him how to think.

John Scott was John Scott Lidgett's maternal grandfather, and it was Scott more than anyone else who influenced Lidgett's educational thinking, both as it was realized in the Bermondsey Settlement and as it formed his attitude to the great educational controversies of the first years of the twentieth century. His aims for the Settlement were six:

1. To bring additional force and attractiveness to Christian works.
2. To become a centre of social life, where all classes may meet together on equal terms for healthful intercourse and recreation.
3. To give facilities for the study of literature, history, science, and art.

4. To bring men together; to discuss general and special social evils and to seek their remedy.

5. To take such part in local administration and philanthropy as may be possible.

6. And so to do all this that it shall be perfectly clear that no mere sectarian advantage is sought, but that it shall be possible for all good men to associate themselves with our work.

These aims he pursued in all available ways, by cooperation with all the local public services and ecclesiastical bodies, and by attracting to the Settlement young residents from the universities who would give part of their career to the education of the under-privileged. The days of Settlements in Lidgett's sense are over, but they have done their share of developing the educational and social consciousness of the Church and nation.

When a national system of popular education was at last introduced in 1870, and the school boards were set up all over the country, the voluntary schools run by the Churches continued to receive financial aid from public funds. The Free Churches in the main objected from the start to this 'Dual System', and adopted the view that it was the business of the State to establish a universal structure of education in the course of which each child received non-denominational instruction; they denied that any particular Church was entitled to receive State aid for the teaching of its own tenets. In accordance with this, Nonconformist day schools were gradually closed down and the children transferred to board schools. In 1902 a new Education Bill proposed to abolish the school boards and replace them by local education authorities which would take over the board schools and secular education in the voluntary schools, assist the voluntary schools from the rates, and allow religious teaching to proceed in the voluntary schools as before; it also, for the first time in British history, planned the provision of secondary and higher education.

The Free Churches broke into immediate revolt against this confirmation of the Dual System and of State aid for denominational teaching, and John Clifford, the Baptist, started a campaign of passive resistance which landed many devout Nonconformists in the unfamiliar atmosphere of prison. The Bill nevertheless became law, and the attempt of the Liberal Government in 1906 to repeal it failed. The Dual System is still with us, and shows no sign of an early death.

The position of Methodism in the controversy was equivocal.

It had gradually reduced the number of its schools during the closing years of the nineteenth century, but not to anything like vanishing point. Some of its leaders could see merits in the Dual System, others could see nothing but faults, and especially the fact that thousands of Free Church children had no chance of education except in Anglican schools, where they would be impregnated with the tenets of the Church of England (in spite of the Cowper-Temple clause, which permitted their withdrawal from explicit religious instruction). Scott Lidgett, Methodism's chief spokesman, with Hugh Price Hughes, saw the great value of the 1902 Bill in its provision of secondary and higher education, though he was against the abolition of the school boards and disliked Church schools. Hughes and he tried to preserve the best parts of the Bill and modify the others, and refused to join the extremist campaign of John Clifford. Hughes died soon after the Bill was passed, but Lidgett dealt with the problems of the difficult years that followed in his spirit. On behalf of Methodism he helped to draft and supported the Liberal Bill of 1906, and deplored its rejection. But afterwards he occupied himself with making full use of the benefits bestowed by the development of the national system.

It has been Methodism's policy since those stormy days to hand over its day schools to the State, though some have regretted this in more recent times, but to maintain secondary boarding schools, many of which now have the status of public schools, as the expression of its concern for Christian education; and at the same time to cooperate with other denominations in the improvement of the religious teaching given in the State schools. It played a full part after the Second World War in the production of the 'Agreed Syllabuses' which stood in pleasing contrast to the ecclesiastical acrimony of the past, and sought to turn religious education in the State schools from a dream into a reality.

There was a widespread awakening in the 1950s to the fact that Agreed Syllabuses, despite their merits, had not achieved nearly as much as had been hoped. A radical re-assessment of the purpose and methods of religious education was shared by teachers from all the Churches, and Ronald Goldman, the Congregationalist, with his Piaget-based theories of religious development in the young, and Harold Loukes, the Quaker, with his more sympathetic account of the actual results of work in the classroom, became the patron saints of a movement to build all religious education on the actual experience of the child. This movement has tended to lead to the disparagement of the biblical and Christian content of religious education, in the exaggerated fear that teachers might seek to evangelize their pupils; its positive effects have been an increased respect for non-Christian religions and a desire to arouse and develop a 'religious sense', instead of inculcating a set of propositions.

More recently still, a tornado hit the colleges of education throughout the country, when it was discovered (suddenly, it seemed) by the Division of Education and Science that far fewer teachers would be needed in the schools of the future than the colleges were producing, and that a drastic curtailment of the number and size of the colleges was necessary. From the general *sauve qui peut* which followed (some colleges being closed, others being attached as departments or hostels to polytechnics), Westminster and Southlands, the two Methodist foundations, emerged more or less intact. Both colleges were already co-educational. Westminster remains as an independent college, with a Bachelor of Education degree validated by the Council for National Academic Awards. Southlands becomes a partner in a consortium of colleges in South West London known as the Roehampton Institute of Higher Education. Both will be used for the education of others besides teachers.

Thus Methodism keeps its stake in Christian education, in all senses of that phrase.

The Bermondsey Settlement was to give opportunity 'to discuss general and special social evils and to seek their remedy'. Here Lidgett was giving expression to the permanent Methodist interest in 'social welfare'. Wesley spent much energy in providing for the poor what would now be contemptuously dismissed as 'first aid' but was in fact in his time all that could be provided. Official Wesleyan Methodism continued this policy throughout most of the nineteenth century, but towards its end was beginning to see that some social evils were radical, and could be remedied only by legislative action; hence its growing alliance, unofficial but real, with the Liberal Party. The largest single factor in the degradation of the poorer classes was addiction to 'drink', and though Wesley had not recommended teetotalism, all the Methodist Conferences came more and more to do so, and to press for changes in the law controlling the sale of beers, wines, and spirits.

Such measures seemed to be the only answer to a terrible social evil, the extent of which it is hard to imagine today.

Unfortunately the 'drink problem' is liable to arouse latent fanaticisms in people who take either side of the argument; some of the advocates of 'temperance' (as total abstinence came to be somewhat inaccurately termed) have given the strong impression of being cranks, and have become more crankish when faced by the opposition of those who wish to preserve their pleasures. They have even behaved as if total abstinence were the whole, or the major part, of the Christian Gospel. But the Methodist Church has never, in any of its forms, made total abstinence a condition of membership, and in 1974 the Conference positively stated that moderate drinking is perfectly compatible with Christian discipleship. It has been more strict in the matter of gambling, a practice to which as a Church it has always shown itself to be completely opposed, on the ground that it distributes the wealth of communities and individuals on an unjust principle. It is not, of course, possible to prevent all Methodists from gambling, but any Methodist member who is known to gamble (which means in practice, of course, anyone who succeeds in winning a prize that he cannot conceal) is widely disapproved of.

But the real social concern of Methodism, historically and at the present time, is not with these or any other particular issues, on which differences of Christian opinion are known to exist, but with the just ordering of society, national and international. This is the issue which Scott Lidgett had in mind when he stated the aims of the Bermondsey Settlement. This is the issue in all the manifold forms and shapes which it takes in the swiftly-changing modern scene, which the Church's Division of Social Responsibility constantly brings before the Methodist people. Under the guidance of farsighted Secretaries (the names of Henry Carter, E. C. Urwin, Maldwyn Edwards, Edward Rogers and Kenneth Greet are known far outside their own communion), it has issued, and the Conference has approved, statesmanlike pronouncements on war and peace, nuclear disarmament and the peaceful uses of atomic energy, racial conflict and partnership, the Third World, the problems of Southern Africa, industrial relations, and many other burning issues. The popular Press, and even to some extent the serious Press, neglects to report these pronouncements when they are made public. It prefers to maintain the popular image of a Methodist as a holier-than-thou sourpuss, implacably hostile to the harmless enjoyments of the people. And, unfortunately, to this image otherwise competent novelists add their ignorant assent.

None of the Churches has even yet recovered from the shock of the First World War, and Methodism no more than any other. The men in the trenches, and the much smaller number of men who came home from the trenches, asked questions which the complacent but still dominant theology of the Victorian era was powerless to answer. The gaps which appeared in once crowded churches were not all caused by the mass slaughter of the war. Becoming gradually conscious of the inadequacy of traditional evangelical theology, with its rigid plan of salvation and its literal adherence to the text of the Bible, Methodist preachers tended in the twenties to swing away to the newly discovered 'liberal' position, which discounted the theology of the Atonement in nearly all its forms, reduced the deity of Christ by heavy emphasis on the 'Jesus of History', treated the Bible as the record of man's progressive discovery of God, and put its hopes in the League of Nations as the harbinger of the Kingdom of God. This approach to the mysteries of the Christian religion certainly brought liberation to many thoughtful people who found the old dogmas hard to accept, but it entirely failed to kindle the imagination or the faith of the multitudes now estranged from the Church. It was during the inter-war period, not after the Second World War, for which the Churches were much better prepared than they had been for the first, that Christianity ceased to be important to the majority of the British nation. The losses of the Churches were to some extent concealed by the Englishman's habit of continuing to do what he has ceased to see the point of doing; but they began to come to light during the Great Depression, when the unemployed felt in an obscure way that the Churches had failed them, and came out into the open when the Second World War destroyed the lifelong habits of the British people.

But though there were thus signs that Methodism was losing some of its hold on the serious members of the middle classes in the twenties and thirties, it did not lack personalities who could influence large numbers of people in the traditional manner of Methodism. Samuel Chadwick, really a survivor of the pre-war era, taught successive generations of lay evangelists in training at Cliff College, in Derbyshire, his distinctive interpretation of the Methodist doctrine of holiness, and outside the college commended the 'simple Gospel' by his obvious embodiment of its ethical precepts. Dinsdale T. Young drew large crowds every Sunday to the Central Hall, Westminster, by his plain and eloquent statement of traditional evangelicalism; he repeated his text so often in the course of each sermon that no one could go away in complete ignorance of his theme. Rather more in tune with the modern spirit was F. Luke Wiseman, who was prepared to go some way in re-stating ancient truths, and was in addition a wise and enterprising administrator of what is known in Methodism as 'Home Missions'. To those freshly awakened to the importance of the historical life and living words of Jesus of Narareth, W. Russell Maltby, with his uncanny knowledge of the human heart, and J. Alexander Findlay, an outstanding scholar in his own right, gave profound and imaginative enlightenment. And there were two men young enough to make as great an impression on their hearers during and after the Second World War as before it, W. E. Sangster and Leslie D. Weatherhead. Sangster combined a large and generous humanity and a resonant and picturesque oratory with no mean knowledge of ethical and philosophical issues. He followed Dinsdale Young at the Central Hall, Westminster, and during the London blitz made it a physical and spiritual refuge for thousands of people. Leslie Weatherhead applied his great practical knowledge of psychology to spiritual problems both in and out of the pulpit, notably while minister of Brunswick Chapel, Leeds, and the City Temple, London; with a style of preaching that was extraordinarily vivid and personal, he obtained a larger following, probably, than any other preacher of the age, and expounded a theology that took full account of modern questioning about the meaning of life.

The greatest event in Methodism between the wars was its reunion. In 1907 three of the smaller Methodist Churches—the Methodist New Connexion, the Bible Christians, and the United Methodist Free Churches—had come together without much difficulty, and formed the United Methodist Church. The idea of one Methodist Church for the whole country came to birth during the next few years, and was actively fostered after the First World War by the responsible leaders of the three great Methodist denominations—the Wesleyan Methodist, United Methodist, and Primitive Methodist Churches; there were some small groups of Methodists who preferred to remain outside the discussions. There was little or no theological difference between the Churches, though the Wesleyans tended to lay greater stress on the Sacraments and the doctrine of the Church, and had a 'higher' conception of the ministry, while the United and Primitive Methodists were more closely akin to historic nonconformity. Certain 'class' differences were also observable. Wesleyans, except for those attending the Central Halls in the industrial centres, tended to belong to the established middle classes, and to be professional people, well-to-do tradesmen, and black-coated workers; United Methodists belonged partly to these classes, but rather more to that of artisans and skilled manual workers; Primitive Methodists, with their origins deep in the mining and heavy industry communities, sprang mostly from the robuster and more enterprising section of the working classes, though many of them were now emerging into the professions. To put it in another way, Wesleyans could afford to send their more brilliant sons and daughters to Oxford and Cambridge, and their able ones to other universities; there were hardly any United Methodists, and even fewer Primitive Methodists, at Oxford and Cambridge, and a slowly increasing number at other universities.

The two smaller Churches were more eager than the largest one to consummate union; their resources were already badly stretched by post-war conditions, and they looked forward to belonging to a larger and more comprehensive communion than they had previously known. The Wesleyans were not so easily convinced of the practical advantages of union, though their leaders, and notably among the laymen Sir Robert Perks, were well aware of the theological need for unity and of the scandal of division. After the United and Primitive Methodist Conferences had voted decisively for the scheme of union, and the 'Representative Session' (ministerial and lay) of the Wesleyan Methodist Conference had done the same, the final issue lay with the 'Pastoral Session' (ministerial) of the Wesleyans. A seventy-five per cent majority was required—and this was exactly what was obtained. A missionary home on furlough from India happened to come into the assembly, where every minister had the right to vote, at the right moment. He voted for union, and his vote settled the matter.

The Uniting Conference was held in September 1932. The new constitution followed traditional Methodist lines, and sought to include the peculiar characteristics of the uniting Churches. The President of the Conference was always to be a minister, but since the Primitive Methodist President had sometimes been a layman, the office of a lay Vice-President was set up. In the Wesleyan Methodist Conference, the 'Legal Hundred', which owed its origin to Wesley, had survived all through history; distinguished ministers were elected to it as vacancies occurred, and remained in it until two years after retirement; this institution found no place in the new Methodism, because the smaller Churches found it a trifle undemocratic, though provision was made for a limited number of ministers and laymen to be elected by the Conference to sit in the Conference for three years consecutively. On the other hand, the session for ministers only, which was lacking in United and Primitive Methodism, was established in deference to Wesleyan Methodist wishes. The details of the Constitution were inclined towards Wesleyan Methodist procedures, but the doctrinal clauses in the Deed of Union (required by the Methodist Church Union Act of 1929) allowed sufficient liberty of interpretation to satisfy all types of Methodist thought.

The effect of union on the higher reaches of the Church was profound and immediate. The administrative departments and the funds were unified, missionary activity was coordinated, Kingswood School and its sister school, Trinity Hall in Southport, became available to the children of all ministers, and the theological colleges began to train a succession of ministers from all three traditions, to whom the differences between them became more and more irrelevant. The chief offices in the Church were given with strict but voluntary justice to members of all three uniting Churches who had served their communions well in the past. A new *Hymn Book* and a new *Book of Offices* were authorized and published. And when it became necessary, with the passing of the years, to draw up Catechisms and make declarations on matters of Faith and Order, the necessary committees were always chosen with due regard for all theological schools within the Church. For a time there were those who looked carefully to see that the interests of the tradition from which they came were being properly conserved when appointments were made or decisions taken, but that spirit has gradually died out.

But in the Circuits things did not happen so agreeably. In many towns and villages, and sometimes very small ones at that, Wesleyan Methodist, United Methodist, and Primitive Methodist

Churches had stood cheek by jowl, and sometimes had seemed to glare and glower at each other. They provided far too many seats for the needs of the 1930s (and still more of the fifties and sixties), and in most cases the congregations of all could easily have been accommodated in one. Also, a town and its surrounding villages often had two or three Circuits, one for each form of Methodism, and a Minister going to conduct a service in one of the churches in his Circuit might pass three or four which belonged to the other Circuits. One of the main objects of Methodist Union was to reduce this chaos to order. In many places the right thing happened at once: Circuits were amalgamated, expenses were cut down, ministerial manpower was released for urgent tasks in new communities. In other places it happened slowly, but fairly steadily. But in far too many places it did not happen at all for many, many years. When people, accustomed to worship in the same building for fifty years, are reluctant to move away from it, lest 'the spirit should not be the same', and to work closely with other Christians whom they have learned to regard as inferior or 'snooty' it is easy enough to find specious reasons why the work in such and such a church should not be abandoned—it is possible even to make the stupendous effort required to raise the necessary money for redecorating the premises. The Conference was not empowered in ordinary circumstances to close churches or amalgamate Circuits against the wishes of the trustees; all it could do was to refuse to appoint a minister to take pastoral charge of the congregation concerned, and this it was of course reluctant to do. The hope that the processes of mortality would solve the problem was not entirely fulfilled, though in the early sixties there were renewed signs that charity and common sense were beginning to prevail. Meanwhile the needs of a myriad new housing estates cried out for the men and resources which could so easily be made available.

The war of 1939 to 1945 destroyed a large number of Methodist churches, and sometimes the ones that could most easily be disposed with on grounds of redundancy. It destroyed so many other things as well, including the last surviving traces of the nineteenth-century world picture, that the period since it finished has been one of major reconstruction. All the things that have happened in the Methodist Church in the last three decades are to be viewed as attempts, some successful and some not, to weave again the fabric of Church life and thought, with a proper sense of continuity with the past, but with an equal sense of the newness and urgency of the modern situation.

During the war the resources normally available to the Church itself had to be largely diverted to the purposes of national survival, to the preservation of elementary decencies and principles, and to the material and spiritual care of those actually involved in hostilities. In many ways the Church emerged from the ordeal strengthened rather than weakened—more aware, for instance, of the thoughts coursing through the mind of modern man, and of its deficiencies in dealing with them, more willing to use a contemporary approach to the problems of the rising generation, less complacent over the way things had always been done and the truth had always been expressed. Numerically, the gaps in the ranks had been exposed rather than increased (except by actual casualties). In 1939 the official membership was just over 800,000; in 1946 it had fallen to 745,000. In 1961 it was 729,000, but this number included far more younger members than a few years previously. But by 1974 the number had declined to 550,000.

The first post-war task was physical reconstruction. The expense and labour involved were of fantastic dimensions, but were greatly reduced by Government cooperation and subvention, and by the fact that all the Churches worked together in the most friendly fashion through the Churches' Main Committee. Credit on the Methodist side must be given to E. Benson Perkins and his colleague in the Chapel Department, Albert Hearn, for straightening out the problems of those difficult years with zeal and enterprise. The first new buildings, because of severe restrictions on expenditure and the use of building materials, were planned on simple, conventional and pseudo-Anglican lines. But as more money and more fruitful ideas became available, the architects employed by Methodist trustees (under the guidance of the Chapel Department) were encouraged to be more adventurous, and have produced several striking contemporary churches. In the new communities on the edge of the great cities, as in Wythenshawe near Manchester and Filton near Bristol, churches full of light and air, with a beauty of their own and an adaptability to all modern needs, have been built. Rebuilding is not so necessary or so easy in more established communities, but the Punshon Memorial Church in Bournemouth (designed by Ronald H. Sims), which was locally expected to resemble a jam factory, with its functional-looking rectangular structure and its exquisitely thin and lofty spire, in due course won the loud approval of impartial experts. Very rarely in modern Methodist churches is the pulpit to be found in the central place in which the Victorians and Edwardians put it. It is quite clear that congregations will never again be found for the grim structures of many parts of North Country Methodism, nor probably for the neo-Gothic creations of the Wesleyan Methodist bourgeoisie. The Methodist Church is beginning to come to terms with this fact; it is also more concerned to build for worship as well as for preaching and is beginning to apply the lessons of the Liturgical Movement to its architecture.

Something like one church, church hall, or school hall was opened on the average every two and a half days by the Methodist Church during the later years of the fifties. This would have been impossible without the munificence of the Joseph Rank Benevolent Trust, endowed by a great Methodist industrialist and willing to help any cause that can be shown to be evangelistic in purpose.

The process of church-building slowed down in the sixties. And the age of the multi-purpose church building arrived. It became obviously uneconomical to put up and maintain, and heat, a 'sanctuary' which was going to be used for three hours in the week at most. There seemed to be no good theological reason for doing so either, and contemporary liturgical thought positively asked for churches with a more flexible use. So a number of Churches began to be built which are simple in design, contain a movable Communion Table and chairs instead of pews, and can be used for many occasions other than those of worship. A notable example is the chapel of Wesley College, Bristol.

Even more important than the reconstruction of buildings is the reconstruction of theology. A long line of Methodist Biblical scholars had prepared the way for this. W. F. Moulton (1835–98) played a large part in the preparation and publication of the Revised Version. His elder son, James Hope Moulton, became a great authority on the Egyptian papyri—which caused the kind of stir when they were discovered which the Dead Sea Scrolls have caused in our own day—and was responsible for a standard Grammar of New Testament Greek and (with G. Milligan) for an equally standard Vocabulary of the Greek Testament. He was killed in a ship torpedoed in the Mediterranean in 1917. A. S.

Peake (1865–1929), a layman who taught many generations of Primitive Methodist ordinands at Hartley College, Manchester, and became the first Rylands Professor of Biblical Criticism and Exegesis at Manchester University, did as much as any one man to introduce Methodists to the critical approach to the New Testament, and to show them that it was wholly consistent with deep loyalty to the historic Christian faith. The one-volume Commentary on the whole Bible which he edited became an indispensable aid to theological students. W. F. Lofthouse wrote an outstanding commentary on Ezekiel, but was equally versed in New Testament theology, dogmatics, the philosophy of religion, and the social and economic significance of the Gospel. W. F. Howard, who followed Lofthouse as Principal of Handsworth College, brought out illuminating studies of St John's Gospel; and Vincent Taylor did the same for the Synoptic Gospels, and also wrote extensively on New Testament theology. Norman Snaith and George Anderson have made large contributions to the study of the Old Testament and its theology. W. F. Flemington (in his *New Testament Doctrine of Baptism*), C. Kingsley Barrett (most of all in his commentary on St John), C. Leslie Mitton, Kenneth Grayston and Morna Hooker, the first woman and the first layperson to become a Lady Margaret Professor of Theology in Cambridge, have handled the New Testament with similar skill.

It is not surprising that when Methodist teachers sought to meet the needs of the post-war age by replacing the individualistic, over-optimistic, rather uncertain theology of the thirties by something better and truer, they looked for a Biblical theology. In the uncertainties of the times, many in all the Churches were taking refuge again in the old infallibilities of Church and 'verbal inspiration'; most Methodists went rather to dominant themes of the Bible, revealed even more clearly by critical research as our primary witness to the Word of God made flesh. In this they were greatly helped by the fresh light thrown on the Reformation by Methodist historians like Philip S. Watson and E. Gordon Rupp, who were the first to make available in English and interpret to the English-speaking world the new Continental studies of Lutheran theology, itself a rediscovery of the Bible as the Word of God. Without abating in the least the Methodist emphasis on the prime necessity of personal religion, the personal knowledge of God through conversion, and the quest for holiness, Methodist preachers began to proclaim once again the Biblical doctrine of the Kingdom of God, made present and visible in the life, teaching, death, and resurrection of Jesus Christ, and to be fulfilled by His coming in glory. They also reasserted the doctrine of the Church as it is found in Scripture. Especially valuable at this point were the writings of R. Newton Flew (particularly *Jesus and His Church*), who combined acute New Testament scholarship with a wide knowledge of ecumenical thought and movements; while Frederic Greeves revived interest in the Biblical conception of sin, and A. Raymond George has explored a field unfamiliar to Methodists, liturgical theology. Not all of these names are well-known outside the Methodist communion, but it is the habit of Methodist Ministers to revere (perhaps unduly) their tutors in the Gospel, and so their influence has been profound in their own Church.

In some ecumenical circles it is held that Methodism is more notable for its warmheartedness than for the depth and width of its theological thought. It is true that Methodist theologians of the last half century have not made the contribution to creative theological thinking which their learning and wisdom have given good grounds for expecting. One reason is certainly that a comparatively small Church is bound to employ its scholars so heavily in teaching and administering that they have little time left for undistracted study and meditation. In spite of this, several of them have played a part in the formulations of ecumenical consensus by the World Council of Churches and its Faith and Order Commission, mediating sometimes between extreme 'catholics' and extreme 'protestants'. And on the American Scene works of great importance stand to the credit of Albert C. Outler, with his immense range of historical and theological expertise, John Deschner, who has branched out into many theological fields from his study of Wesley's thought, and John Cobb, who has reinterpreted A. N. Whitehead in his 'process theology'.

The wave of radical theology which, unleashed by Bishop Robinson's *Honest to God*, swept over British and American Christianity in the sixties, did not by any means leave Methodism untouched. In Britain the radical Methodists mostly belonged to the Renewal Group, comprised of younger ministers and lay-people. Negatively, they reduced the Christian Faith to its bare essentials, and sometimes, it seemed, further still, though they did not announce the death of God; they called into question many received doctrines and practices, and reposed little faith in traditional formulae or in the Methodist establishment. Positively, they redirected the attention of the Church to Jesus, the servant and the man for others; they clamoured for a secular theology; they saw the face of Christ in suffering humanity; and they showed that the Biblical doctrine of salvation embraces all parts of human life and society. Their denials and arguments gave new life to theological discussion among students and ministers, and a greater urgency to social action; and although the impact of radicalism gradually weakened in the seventies, it has left a definite mark on Methodist thinking in the form of a greater concern for contemporary realities and intelligible religious language.

The growth of closer relations with other Churches, as well as its own internal needs, has forced the Methodist Church to formulate its doctrine of the ministry and of ordination. The official Conference statement of 1960 claims that Methodist ministers have the same office within the total ministry of all Christian people as was exercised in New Testament times by the 'presbyters', or 'elders', who were at that time also called 'bishops'. They are 'Ministers, not of the Methodist Church only, but of the Holy Catholic Church'. Without a divine call to the ministry 'no man can be a true minister of the Church'. When a man has been ordained he exercises his ministry as Christ's ambassador and 'the representative of the whole people of God'; by virtue of his office he has 'full authority to administer the Sacrament of Holy Communion'. He has a 'principal and directing part in those spiritual activities, preaching the Word, and pastoral care, which he shares with lay members of the Church. In the office of a minister are brought together the manifold functions of the Church's ministry'.

In the sixties and early seventies the nature and authority of the ordained ministry have continued to be a matter of discussion and controversy in the Methodist Church, as elsewhere. At the same time, a new emphasis has been placed on the ministry of the laity—mentioned, indeed, in the 1960 Statement, but still needing to be expounded and practised at greater depth.

Methodists constantly remind each other that they are committed to the view that the ordained minister does not possess any priesthood that he does not share with the whole company of Christ's faithful people; and this indeed is laid down in the doctrinal clauses of the Deed of Union agreed at Methodist union. Does this mean that a minister differs from the other members of 'the priesthood of all believers' simply in the respect that he has different functions that he performs? If so, then the 'office of a minister' is just the sum of the functions that he performs; and in Methodism the only function that a minister has which a layman does not have is that of presiding at the Holy Communion (and a layman can have even that by special dispensation).

On the other hand, is the doctrine of the universal priesthood consistent with the notion that a minister by nature of his ordination belongs to a different, higher order of priesthood than his lay brethren and sisters? Such a notion smacks of sacerdotalism to most Methodists.

The official Conference Statement on Ordination of 1974 settles for a view which is neither 'functional' nor 'sacerdotal', neither particularly 'high' nor particularly 'low'. Following and developing the Statement of 1960, it declares that all members of the people of God, ordained and unordained, are called 'to be the Body of Christ to men. But as a perpetual reminder of this calling . . . the Church sets apart men and women, specially called, in ordination. In their office the calling of the whole Church is focused and represented, and it is their responsibility as representative persons to lead the people to share with them in that calling. In this sense they are the sign of the presence and ministry of Christ in the Church, and through the Church to the world.'

Until comparatively recent times, a Methodist minister was expected to spend all his time within his own Circuit, carrying out his liturgical, pastoral and administrative duties; and indeed there was plenty for him to do. This conception dies hard in Methodism, though it has become slightly absurd as well as impracticable. It has long been necessary to take ministers from the Circuits to administer the Church, to teach ordinands, and to act as service and school chaplains. Since the Second World War they have broken out into many other valuable jobs, in the furthering of the ecumenical movement, in university, college and school teaching appointments, in the social services and industry. If Methodism was to fulfil its traditional missionary function in a society where large areas of human life lay wholly outside the scope of its normal working, it was clearly necessary to second some ministers to these appointments. At first the Conference, in a somewhat patronizing manner, 'permitted them to serve external organizations'.

But this was a quite inadequate provision, and in the late sixties it was agreed to experiment with 'ministers in the sectors' —the 'sectors' being the areas of life outside the Church where a true Christian ministry can nevertheless be fulfilled. 'Sector ministers' receive their income from those who employ them in their sector, but remain subject to the discipline and authority of the Church.

Many Methodists are still not happy about this development, partly because it conflicts with the traditional concept of the Methodist ministry, partly because there is a shortage of ministers for the Circuit ministry, and partly because of the feeling that laypeople can exercise a ministry in the sectors as effective as that of an ordained minister. But it is fairly certain that 'sector ministers' have come to stay, though the name may need to be changed.

Yet the most striking development in recent years has been the ordination of women. The Conference had declared a long time ago, in 1939, that there were no theological objections to this, but it continued through the forties, fifties and sixties to regard the practical difficulties as too formidable for action to be taken. One such difficulty *was* formidable: the prospect of union with the Church of England made it undesirable to go ahead with the ordination of women while negotiations were still proceeding, in case that Church should call off the union because of it. But when the Church of England failed to accept the Scheme of Union (and was, in any case, beginning itself to take seriously the notion of 'women priests'), the other practical difficulties melted away at the same time, and the first women were ordained to the ministry in 1974. Since then, women ministers are coming to be accepted quite naturally by the Methodist Church at large, and the whole, long controversy now seems unnecessary.

The increased challenge to Christianity at all levels, and the shrinking of economic resources, have made it more than ever necessary to put the training of the ministry in the very highest category of importance. The training of a Methodist ordinand is in any case gruelling. He—and now, she—must first become a local preacher, and then offer himself as a candidate for the ministry to local, District and Connexional bodies. During this process he sits for several examinations, and preaches and writes a number of sermons. The final ordeal of candidature is an oral examination by the so-called July Committee (meeting in April), which makes its recommendation to the Conference. If accepted, the candidate is allocated to a theological college. He has a little choice in the matter of colleges, but not much, and the colleges are part of a central organization, though they have much independence of administration. Those who have university degrees or qualifications proceed to study for a degree in theology (the number of these has grown in recent years, though perhaps not quite so quickly as had been hoped); the others take a course specially designed by the college for their needs, and in some ways more comprehensive and pastorally useful than a degree course can be. After leaving college the ordinand must spend a further period of 'probation', that is, of guided study, and supervision by the Superintendent of his Circuit before ordination.

There have been large changes since the Second World War in the content and method of ministerial training. The basic subjects remain the same—Old Testament, New Testament, Systematic Theology and Church History. But philosophy, psychology, pastoral (or 'practical') theology and social studies have been added, and are regarded as integral to the whole. The length and complexity of the curriculum have been achieved at the cost of much of the time that used to be spent on Greek and Hebrew, but the gain probably outweighs the loss. There is much more 'tutorial' and personal teaching, and opportunity for self-expression; above all, theoretical and practical training (the latter gained mostly in neighbouring circuits) are intertwined throughout the four years' course, and chiefly in the later years.

About half of the men who come into college are married, and many have children; many more are married during the course of training. Some problems are, of course, thus created. But the overall effect is to turn college life into a much more human affair than it used to be, and children playing on the campus increase the family atmosphere. Perhaps also the students and their wives become more aware, in good time, of the pressures that will be exerted on both when they enter on the ordinary life of the ministry.

The intense and laudable interest which Methodists take in the training of their ministers is shown by a passionate and painful controversy which continued recently for ten years about the future of the theological colleges. Because of the shortage of candidates for ordination, and because of the shortage of money in an inflationary period, the six colleges which existed in the early sixties were steadily reduced in number. Wesley College, Headingley, Leeds, was amalgamated in Bristol with Didsbury College to form Wesley College, Bristol. As an ecumenical venture of great importance, Handsworth College, Birmingham, was united with the Anglican Queen's College in that city to form The Queen's College, Birmingham. Richmond College, Surrey, after much heart-searching, was closed. This left Wesley House, Cambridge (which because of its connection with Cambridge University and the great potentialities thus provided was deemed invulnerable), Wesley College, Bristol and Hartley Victoria College, Manchester.

One of the last two had to be closed and its premises sold. But which? Hartley Victoria College was rich in the traditions of Primitive Methodism, was the only college left in the north, and had close connections with Manchester University; but its buildings were mostly Victorian, and needed large sums for renovation and modernization. Wesley College embodied the traditions of two earlier colleges, was closely connected with Bristol University, and was the only college left in the south; its buildings were post-war, and a new chapel and teaching facilities had just been added.

The Conference debated the issue for several years in succession, and emotions inside and outside the Conference ran deep and high. In the end, the Conference, after veering in the opposite direction for a while, decided by a narrow majority to retain Wesley College, Bristol, and to sell the property of Hartley Victoria College. Fortunately it has been possible to maintain the presence of a few theological students in Manchester in concert with the Baptist College there.

With a fresh look at theology and theological training came a new concern for the improvement of public worship. A reconstruction of Methodist ideas and practice in this matter was long overdue when the Conference of 1958 appointed a Commission to go thoroughly into the whole subject. In too many churches the tradition of extempore prayer, which is dear to all generations of Methodists, had degenerated into the long-winded repetition of clichés, utterly remote from the needs of the people or the faith of the Church; and the friendly 'togetherness' of Methodist congregations, which is equally precious, had been made into an excuse for casualness and slovenliness. During the fifties, there was a welcome revolt against all this, especially among student congregations and ministers of the rising generation. In particular, attendances at the Sacrament of Holy Communion increased. The Commission's Report was approved in 1960. It recognizes the existence of two main schools of thought in Methodism—that which prefers 'free' worship and that which esteems liturgy more highly—but it sees no final contradiction between them, and recommends measures which will help both, declaring that 'without the enlivening operation of the Holy Spirit' all forms of worship 'are dead'.

But this was only the prelude to a far-reaching liturgical reform undertaken under the inspiration of the movement for liturgical renewal which involved nearly all the Churches of Christendom in the fifties and sixties. In 1962 the Conference asked the Faith and Order Committee to revise the *Book of Offices* over a period of years. It soon became obvious that no mere revision of an existing book would meet the case. All the services needed to be re-written—and the Conference agreed that this should be done.

The doing of it needed more than a decade. Under the direction of Raymond George, but with the active participation of many others with varying degrees of expertise, and in constant consultation with other Methodist Churches and the liturgical Commissions of other Churches, the work was divided out and executed step by step. The first publications which the Faith and Order Committee persuaded the Conference to approve were services for experimental use throughout the Church. During the experimental period many changes—though none of a very radical nature—were suggested from all parts of the Church, and a number of these were incorporated in the final versions which were authorized by the Conference of 1974.

The new *Methodist Service Book*, the use of which is authorized, but not prescribed, contains the Sunday Service, which is the revised order of Holy Communion, for use as the normal Sunday morning service, if desired, Baptism, Confirmation (or Reception into Full Membership), Ordination,

Marriage, and Burial or Cremation. It also contains, of course, the Covenant Service, the only service peculiar to Methodism, and now widely used beyond it. The Lectionary and Collects are also included, and so is the Cranmerian 1936 Order of Holy Communion for those who wish to continue to use it.

The marks of the new liturgies, in Methodism as elsewhere, are the recovery of the fourfold pattern of the Eucharist which comes down from the Early Church, the stripping away of fussy and sentimental words and practices to gain simplicity, the combination of theological truth with relevance to contemporary needs, and the up-dating of language, not into modern jargon, but into direct and dignified speech. Moreover, a great deal of variety in use is allowed for and encouraged, and, above all, the active participation of the congregation is at all points invited.

Those who are familiar with the revised liturgies of the Church of England will notice great similarities between the products of the two Churches. It is a pity that liturgical revision was not undertaken by the two Churches in concert, but the alternative, that is, consultation, and, when appropriate, imitation, has succeeded reasonably well, since the resultant services are very similar with proper denominational differences of emphasis.

The outsider has probably always thought of the Class Meeting as the characteristic institution of Methodism. In actual fact, there has been a long period in which the classes have either not met at all or met to little purpose. Here lost ground is being regained, the movement for the reconstruction of 'fellowship' (in the Methodist sense) began in Cambridge* and was continued in Oxford, in the very early thirties; since the war the Methodist societies in the universities have divided themselves into 'groups' which meet weekly for discussion and devotion, and something of the spirit of the early Methodist societies is abroad again. This has extended itself in some measure to ordinary churches, and Eric Baker, who as Secretary of the Conference was able to keep his finger on the pulse of the Church for many years, gave a great fillip to this real revival of the spiritual life in his Presidential Address to the Conference of 1959.

* It was in a 'Cambridge Group' that Charles A. Coulson, who did so much to reconcile the claims of Christianity and science in the minds of thoughtful Christians, learned much of the meaning of the Christian faith.

There are many critics within the Methodist Church who say that the machinery of its organization is over-elaborate—the Methodist central offices in Westminster have sometimes been called the Methodist Kremlin—and it is certainly possible to be so entranced with the smoothness of the proper procedure—or so irritated by its delays—that the purpose of it all is forgotten. Others reply that a complex organization is needed to meet an exceedingly complex situation. Two post-war changes in administration have tended to greater pastoral effectiveness, and on the whole to greater simplicity. For much more than a century Methodist ministers changed their circuits every three years with extreme regularity. This is a system which had more advantages than appear at first sight. It ensured that no congregation came to depend entirely on a particular pastor or preacher for its growth in grace and the spiritual life; the community had to have a life of its own which persisted through changes of minister. The itinerancy has also done more than anything else to weld the Methodist Church into a unified whole. But it imposed terrible hardships from time to time on the wives and families of ministers and sometimes on ministers themselves, and congregations often suffered harm from the lack of continuity. After the First World War the three years' span gradually turned into one of four or five years; and now five years is the normal minimum term.

The Chairman of the District is a comparatively recent growth in Methodism. When the Church in Britain was organized into Districts, each with its Synod, a Chairman was plainly required. But at first he did little more than preside over the sessions of the Synod, and of course had a normal pastoral charge in addition. Then when some Districts became more heavily populated, or required special care, their Chairmen were 'separated' from ordinary pastoral charge, and given more and more District responsibilities. In the 1950s it was clearly impossible for any Chairman with a pastoral charge to do both his jobs efficiently; in 1957 the Districts were reduced in number, and all the Chairmen were 'separated'. Now at last the Chairman can be 'the pastor of the pastors', and give leadership in evangelism and devotion to this whole District. There were some who opposed this reform, largely on the ground that Methodist Chairmen were now being modelled on Anglican bishops; others were not worried if this turned out to be the case, so long as 'the care of all the churches' was better carried out. No one now wishes to reverse this reform.

Women have played an outstanding part in Methodism from the beginning, and there were ordained women ministers among the Primitive Methodists for a number of years. A company of deaconesses, trained at the Deaconess College, once in Ilkley, now in Birmingham, grapples with heavy tasks of evangelism and pastoral supervision. The number of women Local Preachers has grown considerably, and except in the eyes of anti-feminists their merit is no smaller than that of their men colleagues. The Women's Fellowship embraces women's organizations of all kinds throughout the length and breadth of the Church, providing inspiration and instruction for their leaders. No one needs to be reminded of the pivotal position of ministers' wives; economic necessity, as well as a sense of vocation, nowadays impels many of them to work as day-school teachers and in other jobs, but at a time when many of them are highly qualified to pursue independent careers this can easily be an enrichment for wife, husband and church.

The men of Methodism have been slower to organize themselves than the women, but the formation in the fifties of the group called the Westminster Laymen held out the promise that a new period of fruitful cooperation between ministers and their laymen was opening. The result chiefly to be desired was that the minister should be set free from the accumulating business of administration—in the form of buildings to be cared for, schedules to be filled in, money to be raised—for the work to which he was ordained. This was also one aim of the numerous 'Stewardship Campaigns' of the sixties and seventies which urged people to look upon their time and talents, as well as their money, as a trust from God, not a possession to be used solely for themselves.

As the sixties proceeded, most large-scale organizations in Britain, from the central administration downwards, felt themselves obliged to consider total reorganization in the interests of economy and efficiency. The Methodist Church, with its complex machinery which was becoming more and more expensive while its real income was declining, could scarcely refrain from 're-structuring' itself. Simultaneously with the advent of Kenneth Greet to the Secretaryship of the Conference in succession to Eric Baker, the President's Council came into being. The

Presidency of the Conference, the highest office in the Church, changes hands every year, and exists on a certain lonely eminence, apart from the constant advice of the Secretary. Continuity in policy is hard to achieve, and the President's Council should be able to provide this. The multifarious departments of the Church's bureaucracy were next concentrated into seven 'Divisions'. And then the Councils and Committees at District, Circuit and local level were reduced in size and frequency of meeting, while the introduction of lay-chairmanship was encouraged over a large area of activity.

The coping stone was placed on the process of re-structuring by the coming into operation of the Methodist Church Act, 1976. In two main provisions it marks changes from the Methodist Church Union Act of 1929. (*a*) The management of Methodist property, nearly all of which belongs ultimately to the Conference, is transferred from local trustees to the local Church Councils: this ensures that it is carried out by those actually responsible for the living activities of each church (trustees, on the other hand, were appointed for life, and as they grew older tended to resist the changes indicated by contemporary needs). (*b*) The doctrinal clauses, which are not altered from those of 1929, are now alterable after a fairly elaborate process which ensures mature consideration, by the Conference, and, not as previously, by Parliament only. (Thus the Church becomes free of the State in the matter of doctrine, and more truly a Free Church.)

Both these provisions were plainly acceptable to the great majority of Methodists, but small groups, at great expense to the Church and themselves, carried relentless opposition into Parliament itself. They defended the rights of local trustees (which were, in fact, not so great anyway as many imagined); and they objected even to the *possibility* that any doctrine which had been agreed to in 1929 as a basis for union between the three Methodist Churches should ever be changed by the Church. But their protests failed to convince either the Conference or Parliament.

All these changes so far affect the inner organization of the Church. They are finally justified only if they enable it to make a more effective impact on the world outside. The older methods of evangelism no longer succeed as they did, though they cannot yet be entirely abandoned. It cannot be said that any Church has found anything startlingly or even moderately successful to take their place. In common with other communions, Methodism has tried to take advantage of all the various means of mass communication and to give them a distinctively Christian use. William Gowland's School of Industrial Evangelism at Luton, to prepare men and women to play a Christian role in industry, brings steady results in the training of ministers and lay people to speak about the faith in intelligible terms. There is still no Christian minister who commands the attention of non-Churchmen more than Donald, now Lord Soper, minister for many years of the Kingsway Hall in London. His significance in the Church of today—shown in a picturesque form by his unfailing appearance on Tower Hill and in Hyde Park each week to answer any questions put to him—is that of a man who sees and expounds Christianity in the whole context of social, industrial, and international relationships. It was this vision which motivated his Order of Christian Witness whose members conducted many urban campaigns, and it is this which makes him still, in the House of Lords, a persuasive advocate of Christian Socialism. Following hard in his footsteps is Colin Morris, with an even more contemporary message and a great command of vivid expression. Both Soper and Morris have made notable use of radio and television for saying what they want to say.

The most solid of many expressions of Methodism's concern for mission is in its numerous youth clubs. Before the State took an active part in promoting the service of youth, the Methodist Church was in the field, and the Methodist Association of Youth Clubs has steadily advanced and consolidated its work. It has to be acknowledged, however, that the day of the large church youth club whose members file into church on Sunday evenings, is over; the leaders of youth clubs, whether sponsored by churches or not, now have the exacting task of coping with the large youth population that has little use for the church and often still less for organized society in general.

Sunday Schools, which declined sharply at one time under the impulse of changing social habits, have now reached a steady level, though they still find it difficult to retain their members when they have once reached the secondary school stage. It has at last been widely appreciated that the experts are right who have insisted for many years on the importance of integrating the Christian education of children into the worship and community life of each Methodist Society, and many improved 'Junior Churches' and Family Services are the result.

The policy towards the Church overseas has changed even more rapidly than domestic policy, and no one can foresee what further changes the development of the new nations in Asia and Africa and the West Indies will require. The most obvious change so far is the switch-over from missionary to national leadership. The Methodist Church of Ghana became independent of the British Methodist Conference in 1960, and many others have speedily followed suit. They are all working out their relationships with the Mother Church in a spirit of great affection. The Methodist Church at home and abroad is committed to the policy of partnership between races in every part of communal life, and this means not only unqualified opposition to apartheid, but also the repudiation of paternalism in all its own dealings.

Two world movements touch the Methodist Church in this country so closely that, from a human point of view, they will determine its future. The Methodist Church of Great Britain and the Methodist Church of the United States went their separate ways for a century and a half. It is true that from 1881 onwards an 'Ecumenical Methodist Conference' was held every ten years (except during periods of war); but this was just a speech-making assembly, held for a few leaders who came to know each other quite well. Then, after the Second World War, the movement suddenly came to life, largely at the impulse of two Americans from the Southern States, Bishop Ivan Lee Holt and Elmer T. Clark. In 1947 a Conference was held at Springfield, Massachusetts; there was a strong British delegation, and small ones from many other Methodist Churches. More representative was the Conference at Oxford in 1951, and more representative still that at Lake Junaluska in North Carolina in 1956. The Oxford Conference brought into being the 'World Methodist Council' (the word 'ecumenical' being relinquished to a greater movement still). Since 1951 there has been an ever-growing exchange of ideas, pastors, and teachers, and Conferences held in Oslo, London, Denver and Dublin have done much to knit World Methodism yet more closely together.

The movement is not free from dangers, some of which have already materialized; it might be dominated by the American and British Churches, to the detriment of the young and vigorous Churches of other continents; it might lead to 'denominational imperialism', and produce a generation of self-consciously Methodist rather than ecumenical Christians. But the possibilities for good are as great as the dangers. The various brands of Methodism can enrich each other in thought and life and devotion. British Methodism has much to learn from American largeness of vision and awareness of new possibilities; American Methodism perhaps something to learn from British insistence on inward religion and careful, Biblical thinking. The missionary policy of all the Methodist Churches can be harmonized. A common outlook on world problems can be seen to spring from Methodist convictions. Above all, Methodists of the whole world, thinking together, can formulate for the benefit of the whole Church their specific contribution to ecumenical thought and life.

The World Methodist movement could therefore enhance the Methodist share in the other, greater world movement. That share is already considerable. In the World Council of Churches the Methodist Church of Great Britain is one of the smaller churches from a small country. But it has provided Philip Potter, from Dominica in the West Indies, to sit in the hottest ecumenical seat of all, the General Secretaryship of the W.C.C. It has also provided Pauline Webb, a Vice-chairman of the Central Committee and Chairman of the committee of the Programme to Combat Racism, notable in her own country and far beyond for her championship of the underprivileged-women, blacks, and 'the poor of the world' in every country. It has also strongly supported the theological, evangelistic and social activities of the W.C.C., not least the controversial Programme to Combat Racism, in spite of the fear that the money raised may not be used for wholly non-violent purposes. In Britain it supports the British Council of Churches as much as any Church does, and supplies Harry Morton as the Council's Secretary.

It can fairly be said that there is no movement towards greater Church unity in which British Methodism has not joined. It is part of the United Church of Canada, of the Church of South India, of the Church of North India (though unfortunately the Methodists of American provenance stayed outside this). In Sri Lanka, New Zealand, Australia, Ghana, and wherever else there is a scheme afoot, Methodists help to draft it.

Most British Methodists are proud of all this, of course. But they have not yet been allowed to enjoy Church union in their own country. After the Second World War there was a great upsurge of ecumenical feeling in many parts of England—though not by any means everywhere. In many places, chiefly large cities such as Manchester and Birmingham and Bristol, relationships between ministers and congregations became so close that an overall scheme to break down the official barriers was urgently called for. (It is necessary to say this, as a legend has gained currency that the Anglican-Methodist Scheme was foisted on unprepared and unwilling congregations and ministers by ecclesiastical potentates.)

The Cambridge sermon of Archbishop Fisher in 1946 furnished the most suitable starting-point. He had suggested that the Free Churches should establish intercommunion with the Church of England by 'taking episcopacy into their system'. The Church of Scotland (not a Free Church!) took up the idea, but the same scheme worked out by Anglicans and Presbyterians miscarried. In England the Methodist Church (but not the Congregationalists or the Baptists), after much consideration, agreed to enter into conversations, and later negotiations, with the Church of England, on the understandings that to 'take episcopacy into its system' did not mean accepting a particular doctrine of episcopacy, and that it would not be asked to break off its relations with non-episcopal Churches in England, or with the Methodist Church in America, to come into communion with the Church of England.

Two teams were formed in 1955, each of twelve, the Methodists under the leadership of Harold Roberts, most eminent of Methodist ecumenists. The first report came out in 1958. It was an interim one, and was approved as such by both Churches. It broke quite new ground in two ways; it suggested that intercommunion was not a sufficient goal—nothing less than organic union was that. And it proposed that the first step towards organic union could be a 'Service of Reconciliation'—where hands were laid by Anglicans on Methodists, and by Methodists on Anglicans, with prayer that the Holy Spirit would give to all whatever was lacking in their ministry; this, it was urged, would bring the churches into full communion with each other, since each would then fully recognize the ministry of the other.

Encouraged by their Churches' provisional approval of its ideas, the Commission proceeded in 1963 to bring out a report which definitely proposed a two-stage method of attaining organic union: the first stage to be initiated by a Service of Reconciliation, the consecration of Methodist bishops, and the arrangement that all subsequent Methodist ordinations should be episcopal ; the second stage to be that of organic union, following a period of growing together. The report was signed by all the Anglican members of the Commission, but there were four Methodist 'dissentients'.*

This report was widely (but not widely enough, as appeared later) discussed in both Churches, and both the Anglican Convocations and the Methodist Conference approved of it by overwhelming majorities. A second Commission, of equal size to the earlier one, was set up to work out the details of the scheme, resolve certain theological and constitutional difficulties, answer certain questions raised in the Churches, finalize the Service of Reconciliation, and draw up an Ordinal for use in both Churches during stage one.

The articulated scheme appeared in 1968, after an intermediate report in the previous year. Now the debate broke out in earnest. The scheme was carefully explained and advocated at every level of Methodist life, and all the decision-making bodies, down to the Circuit Quarterly Meetings, were promised a vote. The ultimate decision rested with the Conference, and here a 75 per cent majority was required for final approval. The self-styled 'Voice of Methodism Association' sprang into existence in order to rally the opposition. In certain parts of the country, notably the north-west, the Voice of Methodism mobilized large numbers to attend their quarterly meeting and vote against the scheme, on the grounds that the Church of England was 'taking over' the Methodist Church, that Methodist principles were being betrayed, and Methodist ministers insultingly offered ordination when they were ordained already. But this misinterpretation, though it carried a fair-sized minority of quarterly meetings, did not persuade any District Synod; and after a full day's debate in the Conference of 1969 the scheme was approved by more than the required majority.

In the Church of England many, both of the Evangelicals

* Professor Kingsley Barrett, Dr T. E. Jessop, T. D. Meadley, Dr Norman Snaith.

and of the Anglo-Catholics, were unhappy. The Evangelicals claimed that the Service of Reconciliation was really an ordination of Methodist ministers (even if the ministers concerned did not think so), and therefore unnecessary. The Anglo-Catholics feared that the Service of Reconciliation was *not* an ordination of Methodist ministers, and therefore inadequate. On these opposite grounds the two groups concerted a joint campaign against the scheme, and proceeded to overstress the strength of Methodist opposition to it. The great central body of Anglicans was unmoved by their arguments, but it suffered from lack of organization.

The Convocations debated the issue in London, simultaneously with the Conference in Birmingham. The Bishops approved the scheme by a sufficient majority; the Lower House did not raise the necessary percentage.

In 1971 the Archbishop of Canterbury and the then President of the Conference, with their Churches' concurrence, agreed that the matter should be put to the test again, before all the steam had gone out of the enterprise. To allay doubts, an official clarification of ambiguous points was published.

In 1972 the story of 1969 was repeated. The Methodist Conference approved the scheme by an overwhelming majority. In spite of the continued support of the Bishops, and a most moving and cogent speech by the Archbishop of Canterbury, Michael Ramsey, the scheme failed to gain the necessary majority in the General Synod, of clergy and laymen, which had replaced the purely clerical Convocations.

It is a sad and sorry tale, and marks the end of British leadership in ecumenical matters. Each Church now subsided into its own concerns, and the vision of a united mission to the nation faded away. Many Anglicans who had supported the scheme, and still favoured it, were reluctant to lead the Methodists once more 'up the garden path', as they phrased it, and the issue of unity seemed to be dead.

But a few gleams of hope appeared. The idealism and charity of Pope John XXIII, and the resolutions of the Second Vatican Council, had brought the Roman Catholic Church into the Ecumenical Movement. There has been subsequently a great growth of understanding between the Roman Catholic Churches and other Churches, and both the Anglican and the Methodist Churches are engaged in careful conversations with Roman

Catholics about the many points at which they find themselves (surprisingly) at one with Rome, and about those on which deep disagreement continues.

The Nottingham Faith and Order Conference of 1964 had encouraged the formation of 'Areas of Ecumenical Experiment'—in which congregations from different communions could live and worship together and make experiments in worship and mission which would not be hampered by a too rigid insistence on denominational rules. The failure of the Anglican-Methodist scheme gave an impetus to the formation and maintenance of such areas, notably in the Bristol and Birmingham dioceses. Now more than sixty in number, they are the foci of real ecumenical progress, though they can operate with entire success only when their denominations are really united.

The Congregational Church and the Presbyterian Church of England came together in 1972 to form the United Reformed Church, and this new Church, with the support of Methodists and Anglicans, called *all* the Churches in this country to engage in talks about the resumption of unity talks—the earlier ones had not included any but Anglicans and Methodists because the others had not felt able to join in.

From these 'talks about talks' sprang the 'Churches' Unity Commission'. This Commission, because of the lessons of the past, and its own varied membership, sought a new way of working, and adopted the method of 'process', carrying itself along steadily from the very first principles. But in 1976, speeding itself up a little, it issued Ten Propositions, asking each Church to respond to each Proposition by Yes or No in 1977.

A covenant is proposed, into which all Churches are asked to enter who will acknowledge each other's members as true members of the Body of Christ, and each other's ministers as true ministers of Word and Sacrament in the Holy Catholic Church; and to agree that all future ordinations should include episcopal, presbyteral, and lay elements.

The Methodist Church stands pledged to the pursuit of organic union. The dominant question for Methodists, and all other English Christians, is whether the Ten Propositions offer the best way forward to that goal. So far the response of Methodism as a whole has been distinctly favourable.

CHAPTER TEN

The Prospects

Methodism has a central position in Christendom—not between Rome and Geneva, for there stands the Church of England, but between Rome and the Society of Friends. And if this seems too large a claim, it can at any rate be seen that it is both a Religious Society and a Church*; in doctrine it is moderate and orthodox; it stands in the Protestant tradition, but is at liberty to accept what it will from the 'catholic' part of the Church; in its Church order it contains both Anglican and Presbyterian elements; in worship it lays equal stress on Word and Sacraments, on liturgy and extempore prayer; it asserts both infant baptism and the necessity of personal faith; it sets each person as a sinner before God, to be saved by the grace of Jesus Christ, and invites him into a fellowship of the redeemed which is embodied both in the small group whose members belong to each other and in the Great Church which dwells in heaven and on earth; it strives both for personal holiness and for the redemption of society. At certain times in its history one or other of all these pairs of complementary truths has been over-emphasized and set at odds with its counterpart; but the history and the essence of Methodism contain them all.

What is its future? Four possibilities can be seen.

It may remain much as it is. In this case, it will improve its worship, its organization, its techniques of evangelism, its ways of raising money, its training of the ministry. It will continue to take part in cooperative enterprise with other Churches, and learn much from them. But it will probably dwindle in size down to a certain point, and then remain constant, protected from further erosion by the compactness of its organization and

* The emphases on the Sacraments, on the ordained ministry and Church order, and on the Holy Catholic Church, are marks of a Church. The emphases on personal commitment, on the fellowship of the Class Meeting, and on the admission of members are marks of a Society. The marks of a sect are, of course, quite different.

the corporateness of its spirit. And its effect on the world outside its walls will probably become less and less.

It may unite with other Free Churches, or at least the United Reformed Church. It is naturally waiting for the outcome of the Ten Propositions, but if the Church of England is unable to respond positively to these, such a union will undoubtedly be proposed (the Baptists' doctrine of Believer's Baptism is liable to keep them out of such a union). This would face Methodism with a stern decision. On the one hand, there is great sympathy on many matters between Methodists and other Free Churchmen. On the other hand, such a union might continue into the indefinite future the lamentable division of English Christendom into Anglican and Free Church.

It may unite with the other Methodist Churches to form a World Methodist Church. This is known to be the plan of some influential American Methodists, and to have support in Britain. It would certainly lead to a great evangelistic drive and bring Methodist teaching and resources together into a very powerful whole. But it would cut off Methodists in all countries from their Christian neighbours, bound to them by strong ties of history and experience, and it would be the enemy of the larger ecumenical movement.

It may come closer to the Church of England, after an interim period of growing together as suggested in the Ten Propositions, and ultimately be united with it and with other Churches that will join in. This sounds to some Methodists like a form of absorption of the smaller Churches by the largest, but it is highly unlikely that the Methodist Conference would agree to it on such terms. Such a union would rather be the creation of a 'new' Church, greater than any of its component parts, but containing the best and most lasting elements of each. It would mean a considerable disturbance of Methodist life, and of ways of doing things which are hallowed by long use; it would mean re-organization at every level. Some valuable things might be lost. But it would continue and develop Methodist worship, order, and fellowship, within the larger body, open Methodist minds to ideas and influences so far not available to them, and enable Methodists to pass on to others what the Holy Spirit has taught them. There would be equivalent changes in the Anglican way of life, not least in its relation to the State (though Methodists no longer press for complete disestablishment). Methodism is both an ex-Anglican Society and a Free Church. It would be able to explain the Free Churches to the Church of England, and vice versa, and so help to make reunion a reality.

The decision between these four courses of action cannot be long delayed. To put off a decision means in the end to adopt the first possibility. Which of the four is most likely to put the spiritual resources of Methodism and the gifts of the Holy Spirit that have come to it at the disposal of the whole Church and the whole world? Is the Methodist Church prepared, if necessary, to die in order to live?

Bibliography

Primary Documents

The Journal of John Wesley, edited by Nehemiah Curnock. Eight volumes, Epworth Press, 1938.
The Standard Sermons of John Wesley, edited by E. H. Sugden. Two volumes, Epworth Press, 1956.
The Letters of John Wesley, edited by John Telford. Eight volumes, Epworth Press, 1931.
The Methodist Hymn Book. Epworth Press, 1933.
Hymns and Songs. Methodist Publishing House, 1969.
The Constitutional Practice and Discipline of the Methodist Church. Methodist Publishing House, 1974.
The Senior Catechism of the Methodist Church. Epworth Press, 1952.
The Methodist Service Book. Methodist Publishing House, 1975.
Conference Statements on Doctrine (all Epworth Press):
The Nature of the Church According to the Teaching of the Methodists, 1937.
Holy Baptism, 1952.
Ordination, 1960.
Church Membership, 1961.
Ordination, 1974.
Anglican–Methodist Unity, Parts I and II. S.P.C.K. and Epworth Press, 1968.

General History

A New History of Methodism, W. J. Townsend, H. B. Workman and G. Eayrs. Two volumes, Hodder and Stoughton, 1909.
History of the Methodist Church in Great Britain, edited by Gordon Rupp, Rupert Davies and Raymond George, volume I, 1965 (volumes II and III in preparation). Methodist Publishing House.

Biography of John Wesley

Brailsford, M. R., *A Tale of Two Brothers*. Hart-Davis, 1954.
Green, V. H. H., *The Young Mr. Wesley*. Arnold, 1961.
Piette, M., *John Wesley in the Evolution of Protestantism*. Sheed and Ward, 1937.

Vulliamy, C. E., *John Wesley*. Third Edition, Epworth Press, 1954.

Theology

Baker, E. W., *The Faith of a Methodist*. Epworth Press, 1958.
Cannon, W. R., *The Theology of John Wesley*. Abingdon Press, U.S.A., 1946.
Lindström, H., *Wesley and Sanctification*. Epworth Press, 1946.
Williams, C. W., *John Wesley's Theology Today*. Epworth Press, 1960.
Davies, Rupert E., *What Methodists Believe*. Mowbray, 1976.

Miscellaneous

Bready, J. W., *England Before and After Wesley*. Harper, New York, 1938.
Davies, R. E. (editor), *John Scott Lidgett*. Epworth Press, 1957.
Edwards, M. L., *After Wesley*. Epworth Press, 1935.
Family Circle. Epworth Press, 1949.
Ives, A. G., *Kingswood School in Wesley's Day and Since*. Epworth Press, 1970
Kent, J., *The Age of Disunity*. Epworth Press, 1966.
Newton, John A., *Susanna Wesley and the Puritan Tradition in Methodism*. Epworth Press, 1968.
Pickering, W. S. F. (editor), *Anglican-Methodist Relations*. Darton, Longman and Todd, 1961.
Rack, Henry D., *The Future of John Wesley's Methodism*. S.P.C.K., 1965.
Rattenbury, J. E., *The Eucharistic Hymns of John and Charles Wesley*. Epworth Press, 1948.
Rupp, E. G., *Methodism in Relation to the Protestant Tradition*. Epworth Press, 1952.
Sangster, Paul, *Doctor Sangster*. Epworth Press, 1962.
Semmel, Bernard, *The Methodist Revolution*. English edition. Heinemann, 1974.
Sweet, W. W., *Methodism in American History*. Revised edition. Abingdon Press, 1953.
Wearmouth, R. F., *Methodism and the Common People of the Eighteenth Century*. Epworth Press, 1945.
Methodism and the Working Class Movements of England, 1800–1880. Epworth Press, 1937.
Methodism and the Struggle of the Working Classes, 1850–1900. Backus, Leicester, 1954.
Weatherhead, A. K., *Leslie Weatherhead*. Hodder and Stoughton, 1975.

Index

Aberdeen, 110
Africa, 15, 142, 145
African Methodist Episcopal Church, 140 n.
African Methodist Episcopal Church Zion, 140 n.
Agreed Syllabuses, 155
Aldersgate Street, 51
Alleghanies, the, 139
Alleine, Joseph, 34
Alleine, Richard, 34, 77
American War of Independence, 109
Andrew, Bishop, 140
Anne, Queen, 22, 24f, 39
Annesley, Samuel, 38
Antigua, 143
Antinomianism, 76f, 89, 92
Apartheid, 145, 178
Arch, Joseph, 132 f.
Areas of Ecumenical Experiment, 183
Arnold, Matthew, 153 f.
Asbury, Francis, Bishop, 136 ff.
Assisi, 16 ff.
Augustine, St., 14
Australia, 142, 148
Austria, 148

Baker, Eric W., 173, 175
Baltimore, 135, 137
Bands, 64
Bangor, 26
Baptists, 117, 143 f., 154, 185
Barnett, S., 151
Barrett, C. K., 165, 181 n.
Barth, Karl, 84
Bath, 22, 64, 115, 152
Baxter, J., 144
Belgian Congo, 146
Belgium, 148
Bell, Andrew, 153
Bell, John, 132
Bengel, J. A., 83
Bennet, J., 54
Berkeley, George, Bishop 29 ff.
Bermondsey Settlement, 151, 153 f., 156
Bernard of Clairvaux, 20
Berridge, J., 68
Bible Christians, 118, 147 f., 159
'Bible Moths', 44
Birmingham, 180, 183
Board Schools, 154
Boardman, R., 136
Bohemia, 16, 19
Böhler, P., 50 ff.
Böhme, J., 34
Book of Offices, 161, 172
Booth, Catherine, 133 f.
Booth, William, 97, 133 f.
Bosanquet, Mary, 71, 91
Bourne, Hugh, 115 ff.
Bournemouth, 163
Bray, Billy, 119
Bray, T., 32 f.
Brechin, Bishop of, 110
Brethren, Church of the, 19
Brevint, D., 93
Bristol, 22, 26 f., 54 f., 57 ff., 69, 78, 108, 110, 118, 180, 183
Broadhurst, H., 131 f.
Bronte, P., 68
Brothers Minor, 17
Brunswick, Georgia, 57
Brunswick Chapel, Leeds, 122, 159

Bunting, Jabez, 121 ff., 130, 143 f.
Burdsall, Mr., 123
Burnet, G., Bishop, 26
Burrington Combe, 75
Burslem, 116
Butler, J., Bishop, 26 f., 30 ff., 52, 64 f., 67, 108

Calvin, John, 34, 74, 148
Calvinism, 28, 74 ff., 80, 85
Calvinistic Methodist Church, 76
Cambridge, 24, 68, 129, 160, 171, 180
Cambridge Platonists, 28 f.
Camp Meetings, 116 f.
Canada, 118, 144, 179
Canterbury, Archbishop of, 26, 29, 64, 117, 182
Carey, W., 143
Carmarthen, 127
Caroline, Queen, 38
Carter, H., 157
Causton, Mr., 48
Central Hall, Westminster, 159
Central Halls, 127, 160
Ceylon (Sri Lanka), 142, 144, 146 f.
Chadwick, S., 158
Chairman of District, 174
Chapel Department, 163
Chapels (Trade Union), 131
Charles II, 23
Charterhouse School, 41
Chartists, 63, 130
Checks to Antinomianism, 69, 76
Chesterfield, Lord, 58
Chile, 142
China, 147 f.
China Inland Mission, 147
Christ Church, Oxford, 41
Christian Citizenship Department, 157
'Christian Library', 34
Christian Socialists, 133
Churches' Main Committee, 163
Churches' Unity Commission, 183
Circuit riders, 136 f.
Circuits, 76, 161 f.
City Temple, 159
Civil War, American, 140
Clarendon Code, 23
Clark, E. T., 178
Classes, Society, 63 f., 102, 131, 134, 141, 173
Clayton, J., 45
Cleckheaton, 121
Cliff College, 158
Clifford, J., 154
Clowes, W., 115 ff.
Cobb, J., 166
Coke, Thomas, Bishop, 110, 137 ff., 143 f., 146
Cokesbury College, 138
Collegia Pietatis, 20 f.
Coloured Methodist Episcopal Church, 140 n.
Combination Acts, 115
Committee of Privileges, 117
Conference, 109, *et passim*
Congregationalists, 104, 113, 117, 147, 183
Connecticut, 110
Conventicle Acts, 64, 117
Convocation, Houses of, 25, 108, 182
Cornwall, 79
Corporation Acts, 24
Coulson, Charles, 173 n.
Convenant Service, 77, 173
Crowther, 123
Cuba, 142
Cudworth, R., 28
Cumberland, Duke of, 70
Cybele, 13

Deed of Declaration, 109
Deed of Union, 161
Deism, 29 f.
Delamotte, C., 47
Denver, Colorado, 178
Deschner, J., 166
Didsbury College, 171
Dissenters, 13, 23, 31 f., 38, 94, 106 f., 113, 117, 125 f.
Dissenting Academies, 24 f., 26
Dow, Lorenzo, 116 f.
Dual System, 154
Dublin, 178

Dunn, S., 123
Durham, Bishopric of, 26 f.
Durham, County, 26, 132
Dutch Reformed Church, 145

Eckett, R., 124
Ecumenical Methodist Conferences, 178 f.
Edinburgh, 146 f.
Education Bills, 154 f.
Edwards, Maldwyn L., 157
Elizabeth II, 148
Embury, P., 135 f.
Emmanuel College, Cambridge, 34
England, Church of, *passim*
'Enthusiasm', 44, 65
Epworth, 38 ff., 40
Epworth Rectory, 40
Eugene, Prince, 46
Everett, J., 122 ff.
Everton, 68
Exeter, 108

Faith and Order Committee, 161, 172
Falmouth, 72 f.
Fetter Lane, London, 58, 66 f.
Filton, 163
Findlay, J. A., 159
Fisher, G., Archbishop, 180
Five Mile Act, 117
Flemington, W. F., 165
Fletcher, John, 69, 71, 76, 109, 115
Flew, R. N., 166
Florida, 46
Fly Sheets, 123 f.
Foot, I., 183
Formosa, 143
Foundery, The, 66, 69
Foy, Captain, 63, 69
Francis, St., 17 ff.
Franciscans, 18 ff.
Francke, A. H., 20
Frankfurt, 20
Frederica, 48
Freeman, T. B., 145
French West Africa, 145
Freud, S., 84
Friendly Islands, 148

Gandhi, Mahatma, 146
General Synod, 182
George, King, *see* Taufa-ahu
George I, 34
George, A. R., 166, 172
Georgia, 21, 46 ff., 57 f., 135
Gerhardt, P., 20 f.
Germany, 148
Ghana, 145, 178
Gibbon, E., 34
Gibson, E., Bishop, 27
Gilbert, N., 143
Gladstone, W. E., 127
Gloucester, 56 f.
Gnosticism, 13
Goldman, R., 155
Gowland, W., 177
Grayston, K., 165
Green, V. H. H., 43 n.
Greet, K. G. G., 157, 175
Greeves, F., 166
Gregory, 19
Griffith, W., 123
Grimshaw, W., 68
Gwynne, S., 55

Haime, J., 70
Halle, University of, 20 f.
Hamburg, 148
Handel, 99 n.
Handsworth College, 165, 171
Harris, H., 70 f., 76
Harris, 'Prophet', 145
Harriseahead, 116
Hartley Victoria College, 165, 171
Hawkins, Mrs, 48
Haworth, 68
Hearn, A., 163
Heck, Barbara, 135
Herrnhut, 35 f., 58
Hill, R., 75, 97
Hoadly, G., Bishop, 26
Holt, Ivan L., Bishop, 178
'Holy Club', 44 f., 71
Home Missions, 159

Honest to God, 166
Hooker, M. D., 165
Hopkey, Sophia, 48 f., 54
Horneck, A., 31
Horsefair, Bristol, 62 f.
Howard, W. F., 165
Hughes, H. P., 127 ff., 150, 155
Hugolini, Cardinal, 18
Huntingdon, Countess of, 71, 74 ff.
Hus, John, 19
Hyde Park, 177
Hyderabad, 146
Hymns and Songs, 104

Ilkley, 128, 175
Indemnity, Acts of, 23
Ingham, B., 47, 74
Innocent III, 17
Interim Report, 181
Ireland, 67, 125, 135 f.
Italy, 17, 148
Ivory Coast, 145

Jablonski, D. W., Bishop, 36
Jackson, T., 126
Japan, 142
Java, 144
Jessop, T. E., 181 n.
Job, Book of, 38
John XXIII, Pope, 182
Johnson, Samuel, 53, 56, 137
Jones, John, 78 n.
July Committee, 170
Junaluska, Lake 178

Keble, J., 126
Kempis, Thomas à, 34, 42 f.
Kidd, B. J., 15 n.
Kilham, A., 113 f.
King, P., 108 f.
Kingsway Hall, 177
Kingswood, 57
Kingswood Chase, 57, 78
Kingswood School, 78 f., 152 f., 162
Kirkham, Betty, 43
Kirkham, Robert, 43
Kirkham, Sally, 43
Korea, 142

Labour Movement, 130 f.
Lambeth Appeal, 151
Lancaster, J., 153
Lateran Council, 16
Latin America, 142
Latitudinarians, 29
Lavington, Bishop, 72, 108
Law, William, 30 f., 34 ff., 42 f., 52, 72
League of Nations, 158
Lecky, J., 91
Lee, Peter, 132
Leeds, 70, 122, 159
Legal Hundred, 109, 124, 161
Leoni, 78
Liberals, 127, 132, 154
Liberia, 145
Lidgett, J. Scott, 150 ff., 153 f.
Limerick, 135
Lincoln, 27
Lincoln Castle, 38
Lincoln College, Oxford, 43 f.; Rector of, 44
Liverpool, 119, 144
Liverpool, Lord, 117
Liverpool Minutes, 119 f.
Local preachers, 131, 170, 175
Locke, J., 29
Lofthouse, W. F., 165
Lombardy, 16
London, 22, 24, 77, 145, 151; Bishop of, 27, 110
London County Council, 150
Lords, House of, 25, 117
Louis XIV, 135
Loukes, H., 155
'Love Feast', 77
Lucius III, Pope, 116
Luddites, 115, 121
Luther, Martin, 34, 52, 87, 90, 148, 165
Luton, 177
Lyons, 15

Madeley, 69, 109
Madras, 146
Maltby, W. R., 159
Manchester, 70
Manchester Mission, 128

Manners-Sutton, Archbishop, 117
Manning, B. L., 104
Marlborough, Duke of, 46
Maryland, 32, 135
Marylebone, 55
Maurice, F. D., 151
Maxfield, T., 69
Maximilla, 14
Meadley, T. D., 181 n.
Mendeland, 145
Mennonites, 37
Methodist Association of Youth Clubs, 177
Methodist Church Act (1976), 176
Methodist Church Union Act, 161
Methodist Episcopal Church (U.S.A.), 138ff., 142, 178 f.
Methodist Episcopal Church, South (U.S.A.), 140
Methodist Missionary Society, 178
Methodist New Connexion, 113 f., 159
Methodist Service Book, 172
Methodist Times, 127, 151
Methodist Union, 151, 159 ff.
Mexico, 142
Miaos, 147
Milligan, G., 165
Milton, John, 16
Mitton, C. L., 165
Molther, P. H., 66
Montanism, 13 ff.
Montanus, 13 f.
Moravians, 19 f., 35 ff., 47 ff., 58 f., 66, 77, 84
More, H., 28
Morgan, W., 45
Morris, C. M., 177
Morton, H., 179
Moulton, J. H., 165
Moulton, W. F., 165
Mow Cop, 116
Murray, Grace, 54
Murton, 132
Mysore, 146

Namaqualand, 144
Napoleon, 115
Nash, Beau, 64
National Children's Home and Orphanage, 128
National Council of the Free Churches, 127
Nelson, J., 70
New Room, Bristol, 62 f.
New York, 135 f.
New Zealand, 148
Newcastle upon Tyne, 54, 67
Newgate Gaol, Bristol, 60
Newman, J. H., Cardinal, 125
Newquay, 118
Nigeria, 145
Nitschmann, D., 36
Nonconformists, 13, 126
'Nonconformist Conscience', 128 f.
Non-Jurors, 25, 40, 45
Norris, J., 43
North India, 142, 147, 179
Northern Rhodesia, 145
Norwich, 22
Nottingham Faith and Order Conference, 183

O'Bryan, William, 118
Occasional Conformity, 24
Oglethorpe, General, 46 ff., 57
Ohio, 139
Olivers, T., 70
Order of Christian Witness, 177
Ordination Statement (1974), 168
Oriel College, Oxford, 26
Orr, J. E., 125 n.
Osborn, T. G., 152
Oslo, 178
Outler, A. C., 166
Owen, E. C. E., 14 n.
Owen, J., 34
Oxford, 24, 41 ff., 129, 178; Bishop of, 42
Oxford Movement, 93, 126, 134

Pakistan, 179
Palatinate, 135
Parnell, C. S., 128
Pastoral Session, 161
Peake, A. S., 164 f.
Pembroke College, Oxford, 56

Pennsylvania, 37
Perkings, E. Benson, 163
Perks, R., 160
Perpetua, 14
Perronet, V., 68
Peter of Chelcic, 19
Peterloo, 115
Phillips, M., 130
Phrygia, 13 f.
Piaget, H., 155
Piedmont, 16
Pietism, 19 ff.
Pill, 136
Pilmoor, J., 136
Plan of Pacification, 112, 113
Plan of Separation, 140
Poland, 148
Pollard, S., 147
Pope, W. B., 128
Portugal, 149
Potter, P., 179
Preaching Service, 133
Presbyterians, 147, 183
President's Council 175 f.
Primitive Methodist Church, 116 f., 130 ff., 145, 160 ff., 175
Prisca, 14
Programme to Combat Racism, 179
Progressive Party, 151
Protestant Episcopal Church (U.S.A.), 139
Protestant Methodists, 122, 124
Punshon Memorial Church, 163
Purcell, H., 97
Puritans, 25, 28, 33 ff., 74, 80, 121
Pusey, E. B., 126

Quakers, 37, 115 f.
Quiller-Couch, A., 38 n.

Radicals, 115, 120
Rank, J., 164
Rationalists, 29
Rauschenbusch, W., 142
Reform Act, 115, 120
Reformation, 19 f.
Religious Societies, 26, 31 f., 58 f., 61 f., 105, 184
Renewal Group, 166
Representative Session, 161
Restructuring, 175 f.
Richmond College, 171
Roberts, H., 180
Robinson, Bishop J. A. T., 166
Rochester, Bishop of, 115
Rocky Mountains, 140
Rogers, E., 157
Rothe, J. A., 36
Rupp, E. G., 165

Sacheverell, Dr., 25
Sackett, A. B., 152
St. Edmund Hall, Oxford, 75
St. James' Hall, Piccadilly, 127
St. Patrick's Cathedral, Dublin, 99 n.
St. Paul's, Deanery of, 26
Salisbury, 26
Salote, Queen, 148
Salvation Army, 133 f.
Sam's Creek, 135
Sangster, W. E., 159
Savannah, 46 f., 48, 57, 67
Saxony, 35
Scandinavia, 148
Schism Act, 24
Schmidt, M., 37 n.
School Boards, 154
Scotland, 67, 143
Scott, J., 153 f.
Scougal, H., 34, 43, 56
Seabury, S., Bishop, 110
Second Vatican Council, 182
Sector Ministries, 169 f.
Septimius Severus, Emperor, 14
Service of Reconciliation, 180 f.
Sharpeville, 115
Shaw, Barnabas and Mrs., 144 f.
Shebbear, 118
Sheffield, 70
Shoreham, 68
Sidmouth, Lord, 117
Sierra Leone, 144, 146
Simmonds, 47
Sims, R. H., 163
Six Acts, 115, 120
Slavery, 79, 140

Smith, J., 28
Smuggling, 79
Snaith, N. H., 165, 181 n.
Society for the Promotion of Christian Knowledge, 32 f., 105
Society for the Propagation of the Gospel, 33 f., 105
Society for the Reformation of Manners, 33
Sodor and Man, Bishop of, 27
Soper, D. O., 177
South Africa, 144 f.
South India, 146 f.
Church of, 147 f.
Southlands College, 153, 156
Spain, 16, 148
Spangenberg, A. G., 47 f., 66
Spener, P. J., 20
Springfield, Mass., 178
Stanton, 43
Stephens, J. R., 130
Stephenson, T. B., 128
Stillingfleet, E., Bishop, 109
Stoke-on-Trent, 115
Strawbridge, R., 135
Sunday Schools, 141, 152, 177 f.
Superintendents, 76, 109, 121
Switzerland, 148
Sydney, 148

Tasmania, 142, 148
Taufa-ahu (George), King, 148
Taylor, J., Bishop, 34, 42 f.
Taylor, V., 165
Taylor, W., 142
Temple, W., 177
Ten Propositions, 183, 185
Tenison, T., Archbishop, 29
Tertullian, 14
Test Act, 24
Tewkesbury, 26
Theological Institution, 122 f., 124
Thom, W., 113
Thorne, J., 118
Tillotson, J., Archbishop, 29
Tindal, M., 29
Toland, J., 29
Toleration Act, 23, 107, 117
Tolpuddle Martyrs, 130, 132
Tomo-chichi, 46
Tonga, 148
Toplady, A. M., 75 f., 137
Tower Hill, 177
Toynbee, A., 151
Tractarians, 125 ff.
Trevecca, 71, 75
Trinity Hall School, 162
Tucker, J., 72
Tubou, 148
Tunstall, 116
Tuscan hills, 17
Twelve Rules for a Helper, 70

United Methodist Church, 159
United Methodist Free Churches, 124, 146, 159
United Reformed Church, 183, 185
Uniting Conference, 160
University College, London, 151
University of London, 151
Urwin, E. C., 157

Vasey, T., 110, 137
Vazeille, Mrs., 54 f.
Verona, Council of, 16
Victoria, Queen, 146
Virginia, 134
Voice of Methodism Association, 181

Waldensians, 15 ff., 18, 148
Waldo, P., 15 ff.
Wales, 67, 125, 143
War of Independence, American; *see* American War of Independence.
Warren, S., 124
Watson, P. S., 165
Watts, I., 98
Wearmouth, R. F., 131 n.
Weatherhead, L. D., 159
Webb, P., 179
Webb, T., 136
Welch, Mrs., 48
Welsh Presbyterian Church, 76
Wesley, Charles (senior), *passim*

Wesley, Charles (junior), 55
Wesley College, Bristol, 164, 171
Wesley, Hetty, 38 f.
Wesley, John, *passim*
Wesley, Mary, 39
Wesley, Samuel (senior) 38 ff.
Wesley, Samuel (junior) 39
Wesley, Samuel (son of Charles, senior), 55
Wesley, Samuel Sebastian, 55
Wesley, Susanna, 38 ff., 46, 69
Wesley College, Headingley, Leeds, 171
Wesleyan Methodist Association, 124
Wesleyan Methodist Church, 116 f., 120 ff. *et passim*
Wesleyan Methodist Missionary Society, 144 f.
Wesleyan Reform Society, 124
Wesleyan Takings, 123
West Bromwich, 136
West Indies, 144
Western Nigeria, 145
Westminister College, 153, 156
Westminster Laymen, 175
Westminster School, 41
Whatcoat, R., 110, 137
Whichcote, B., 28
Whitefield, G., 27, 56 ff., 70 f., 74 f., 78, 135
Whitehead, A. N., 166
Wight, Isle of, 118
William III and Mary, 23, 39
Williamson, Mr., 49
Wilson, T., Bishop, 27
Wiseman, F. L., 159
Women, Ordination of, 169
Women's Fellowship, 175
Woodward, J., 32
Workman, H. B., 18 n.
World Council of Churches, 179
World Methodist Council, 178
Wright, 38 n.
Wroote, 43 f.
Württemberg, 148
Wyandot Indians, 139
Wythenshaw, 163

Yoder, D. H., 37 n.
York, 82
  Archbishop of, 68, 110
Young, D. T., 159

Zephyrinus, 14
Zinzendorf, Count and Bishop, 19, 36 ff., 58 f., 66